ADVOCACY

A Nurses' Guide

ADVOCACY

A Nurses' Guide

Bob Gates MSc, BEd(Hons), DipN(Lond),
RNMH, RMN, RNT, CertEd.
Lecturer in Nursing, University of Hull

Scutari Press · London

A division of Scutari Projects Ltd., the publishing company of the
Royal College of Nursing

First Published 1994

British Library Cataloguing in Publication Data

Gates, Bob
   Advocacy: Nurses' Guide
   I. Title
   610.73

     ISBN 1-871364-90-6

Photoset by Rowland Phototypesetting Ltd
Bury St Edmunds, Suffolk
Printed in Great Britain

Printed by Hobbs the Printers of Southampton

Contents

Preface

As health care practitioners, nurses spend almost all their time working with people, which places them in the privileged position of being able to observe the frailties of humanity. These frailties become apparent when life events cause people to experience periods of difficulty. Such difficulties may relate to their employment, relationships, housing, or health problems. Clearly difficulty in any of these areas has the potential to affect the achievement of optimal health of the people cared for by nurses. During such life events people may be required to speak up for themselves against some injustice or to safeguard their rights. Some people are unable to speak up for themselves, because of fear of authority figures, ill health (either physical or psychological), learning disability or cultural difficulties. Alternatively there may be problems associated with age; for example, children under the age of 16 are considered too young to represent their own interests adequately. When such a situation arises it is important that people have access to an advocate. An advocate is an individual who is willing to speak up for any person with as much conviction as if that person were one of the advocate's own relatives.

This book is concerned with advocacy and nursing, and its case histories and examples are written primarily for nurses. It is intended to be a resource book that enables students or practitioners of nursing to gain access to information, guidance and direction as to their role in advocacy. The concept and practice of advocacy are not new but the manner in which advocacy is practised differs internationally. The legislative framework within which advocacy operates (Berry 1992) also varies. Therefore it is important for nurse practitioners to understand the complexities and potential problems inherent in the role of advocate. Equally important is the need for nurses to separate their professional and employee roles from any potential advocate role. This is because there are, potentially, large areas of role conflict which nurses may experience if the roles of both advocate and nurse are practised simultaneously. It has been argued that tensions exist when a professional adopts the role of advocate whilst in the employ of the same service agency as the person being represented (Wolfensberger 1972). Conflict of interest may then be inevitable.

Such conflict of interest does not mean to imply that a nurse cannot act as an advocate, for indeed there are many different forms of advocacy. The author challenges the promotion of a simplistic understanding of the concept and practice of advocacy, which assumes that it can be incorporated into the role of a nurse without consequential difficulties. It is relatively easy to suggest the adoption of the role of advocate. Indeed, in its Code of Conduct (UKCC 1992), the United Kingdom Central Council for Nursing, Midwifery and Health Visiting makes advocacy an implied component of a nurse's role. However, there is little in the written word to support a nurse who adopts the role of advocate. It is the author's belief that there has been an attempt by nursing to professionalise advocacy.

The author will identify and clarify how nurses can undertake some aspects of the role of advocate for their patients in such a way as to reduce the threat to their own personal health or professional role. This book will also explain how nurses should 'network' a wide range of advocacy organisations and independent advocates, who may be better placed to serve the interests of their patients. A wide range of literature and case histories is used within the text to provide a springboard for possible further study of more specialised forms of advocacy.

Above all else the author intends to offer a pragmatic approach on how nurses may address the complexity of the practice of advocacy in a range of health and social settings.

References

Berry L (1992) Doing things differently. *Community Care* **30**, 30th April: iii.

UKCC (1992) *Code of Professional Conduct for the Nurse, Midwife and Health Visitor* (3rd edn). London: UKCC.

Wolfensberger W (1972) *Citizen Advocacy for the Handicapped, Impaired and Disadvantaged: An overview*. Washington, DC: The President's Committee on Mental Retardation.

CHAPTER 1

Advocacy and Nursing

This chapter first provides a summary of definitions and different types of advocacy, after which it introduces the reader to some of the inherent problems nurses may encounter, should they adopt such a role. Throughout this chapter contrasting discussion will be offered in order to provide the nurse with a better understanding of advocacy. It is anticipated that the text and case histories provided will facilitate nurses' understanding of their role in relation to advocacy.

The word 'advocate' derives from the Latin 'advocatus' – 'one summoned to give evidence'. The Webster Universal Dictionary (1975) defines advocacy as:

The act of pleading the cause for another.

The way in which advocacy is both defined and understood varies considerably, and this leads to problems in achieving a shared working definition of both its concept and practice. There would appear to be, for example, a professional use of the word advocacy in nursing, which implies that nurses have a duty to act as advocates for their patients. Indeed, there is considerable support in nursing literature for the adoption of this role by nurses (Gadow 1983; Bandman 1983; Healy 1983; Orgel 1983).

By way of contrast, groups such as Advocacy Alliance, an advocacy group to be discussed in chapter 2, restrict the use of the term advocate to that of an independent person who represents the interests of an individual. When advocacy is used within this context the person being represented is often referred to as a protégé or partner.

Another usage of the term lies within some legal

systems. In Scotland and South Africa the term advocate still refers to a barrister. Consequently there often exist legal overtones and connotations within the language of advocacy. Despite these legal connotations, 'pleading the cause for another' is central to any discussion concerning advocacy.

As has already been suggested, the ways in which people understand advocacy differ. The single most important area of difference lies in the distinction between an independent as opposed to a professional advocate. There are considerable tensions resulting from the demands on nurses to fulfil their professional role expectations, their employer's role expectations and the potential role expectations of an advocate. Although some of the problems of acting as advocate are not insurmountable, nurses will inevitably be placed in untenable situations where there is a conflict of interest between these three roles, as will be discussed later in this chapter. However, these tensions make imperative the need for clarity and a working definition of the role of advocate as well as the practice of that role by nurses. If a nurse is able to practise as an advocate, then such a definition must acknowledge the tensions already identified.

The term advocacy within this book refers to:

> The process of befriending and, where necessary, representing a patient, client, partner or protégé* in all matters where the nurse's help is needed, in order to protect the rights or promote the interests of that person. The practice of advocacy must be undertaken in a true partnership, where nurses see these partners as friends and therefore afford them the same care and love as they would to any of their own friends or relatives. Because of the commitments of such a partnership it may be

---

* For the remainder of this text the terms protégé, patient, client and partner are used synonymously.

necessary for a nurse to seek the assistance of an
independent advocate. Such assistance should be sought
when the demands of professional or employer/employee
roles prevent nurses from affording their patients the
requisite degree of care or commitment.

Variations of Advocacy

Legal advocacy

A very specialised form of advocacy is that of legal advocacy. Butler et al (1988) describe it as:

> A process in which legally trained persons pursue and
> represent the rights and interests of people within
> existing legislative frameworks, or they seek to extend
> the parameters of legislation to protect and/or promote
> the rights of an individual.

Clarke (1985) gives an excellent example of this type of
advocacy. The case of Smith, Stringfellow and Poyner
versus Jackson, Blackburn County, was concerned with
establishing the eligibility of people with a learning disability to pursue and exercise their right to vote. In this
case the electoral registration officer would not place the
names of three people who resided at Calderstones Hospital (a large learning disability hospital) on the electoral
role. The electoral officer's decision was based on the
premise that these three persons were patients of an establishment that dealt with the reception and treatment of
people with mental illness or mental defectiveness. He felt
that these three men were 'patients' at this hospital and
therefore they could not be thought of as resident under
the Representation of the People Act 1949. This decision
was challenged and an advocate was sought for the men
concerned, in order that they might be properly represented. Following the court case, Judge Prestt QC, pre-
siding, ruled that although the three men resided within

a hospital they were not receiving treatment for a mental disorder or mental illness. He also concluded that because they were not receiving treatment they could not be classed as patients in the context of the Representation of the People Act 1949, and were, therefore, entitled to have their names placed on the electoral register.

This example demonstrates the complexity of the role of legal advocate and reinforces the need for highly skilled and legally qualified persons. Perhaps it is not surprising that Sang and O'Brien (1984) suggest the practice of this type of advocacy be confined to lawyers and other similarly skilled people, since it is often related to various tribunals and other court case work.

Self-advocacy

In this type of advocacy the advocate, or facilitator, attempts to shift the focus of control from him/herself to the people with whom he/she is working. Williams and Shoultz (1982) define self-advocacy as:

> Individual people or groups speaking or acting on behalf of other people on issues which affect them in the same way as themselves.

In self-advocacy people are encouraged to speak up for themselves, thus bringing about an element of self-empowerment, that is, people speaking for themselves, rather than having an advocate speak for them. There is a strong ideological belief that self-advocacy enables people to grow and develop from the experience of speaking up for themselves. Growth in this context refers to both the enhancement and development of self-confidence and self-esteem. Probably the most widely known text on self-advocacy is that of Williams and Shoultz (1982). In their book they outline the life of a quite remarkable man called Mr Raymond Loomis, who developed a self-advocacy group in Nebraska, North America. The group, called the People First Project, gained national and international recognition. This movement undoubtedly inspired others to follow their example.

Within the UK, an example of a self-advocacy group is recorded by Gates and Lewis (1987). In this example, a group of people at a large learning disability establishment, Leavesden Hospital, was invited to discuss and share ideas and opinions with the curriculum development group of a school of nursing. Their ideas were sought to identify how the course provided for learning disability student nurses could be improved. After the group was formed, a number of issues were discussed and they formed the basis of a range of suggestions that were incorporated into the course. During a six-month period the self-advocacy group grew in confidence and published an article in the hospital magazine. Throughout this period it became evident to the facilitators of the group not only that people with a learning disability were denied equality of rights with other members of society, but also – what was worse – that some members of the hospital team did not perceive people with a learning disability to be worthy of being listened to at all! In self-advocacy it is not just the listening that matters; even more important is the positive response to what is being said.

It may appear somewhat contradictory for a self-advocacy group to have non-disabled members. However, Williams (1989) suggests that almost all self-advocacy groups need non-disabled members in order for the group to become more independent and influential. One consequence of the Leavesden group being involved in the activities of the education department was that it developed into a confident and vocal self-advocacy group and, with further help, organised a national self-advocacy conference – the National Self-advocacy Conference for People with a Learning Disability, January 1987.

Another self-advocacy group is described by Strong
(1992). In this example a Social Education Centre in
Aberdeen established a client committee to bring about
greater self-determination. This committee now shares the
responsibility for the ultimate direction of the Education
Centre.

Despite the very real advantages of encouraging self-
advocacy there is some evidence that there is still much to
be achieved. Sutcliffe (1990) identifies that only 5 out of
64 self-advocacy groups were based in an adult or Further
Education setting.

Collective or class advocacy

Collective or class advocacy (Butler et al 1988), or what
Wolfensberger (1972) refers to as collective or corporate
advocacy, describes large organisations who pursue the
rights and interests of a complete category of people, for
example the Spastics Society or The Royal Society for
People with a Mental Handicap. These organisations have
a national resource that can provide for the appointment
of full-time officers, as well as for the use of volunteers.
Often the work of such organisations is involved in the
promotion of positive imagery concerning the people
being represented, as well as in advocating more enlightened legislation concerning particular groups of people.

Citizen advocacy

Probably the most widely known form of advocacy is
that of citizen advocacy. Heron and Myers (1983) identify
Dolan and Taggart (1972), whom they believe to be the
true pioneers of citizen advocacy. These two people developed a manual on how to secure benefits for disabled
adults. Regardless of the exact date, or who could be said
to be the instigator of citizen advocacy, there is little dis-

agreement that the origins of citizen advocacy lie in the United States of America and in particular with young people with cerebral palsy. At a nationwide American conference of the United Cerebral Palsy Associations (1966), a number of parents who had children with cerebral palsy expressed deep concern for their children's welfare and future. An idea was put forward that the children, after their parents' deaths, could be represented by a citizen advocate, a caveat to the appointment of such individuals being that they would be unpaid citizens who were not connected with the care service provided for the children. Wolfensberger (1983), who suggests that it was this date and group of people which gave birth to citizen advocacy, is the greatest exponent of both its concept and practice. For him, citizen advocacy is primarily concerned with empowering people through an individual relationship, that is one between a citizen advocate and his/her protégé. Wolfensberger (1972) defines a citizen advocate as:

> A mature, competent citizen volunteer representing, as if they were his own, the interests of another citizen who is impaired in his instrumental competency, or who has major expressive needs which are unmet and which are likely to remain unmet without special intervention.

There are, within this definition, two central concepts that require further analysis in order to understand fully the ideological basis of citizen advocacy. Within Wolfensberger's definition he identifies two different types of need which people experience, that is 'instrumental competency' and 'expressive need'.

Instrumental competency refers to those behaviours that enable people to meet the continued demands made upon them by ordinary life situations. Examples of these instrumental competencies are: earning a living, managing financial affairs, accessing education or training, decorating the house, loading a washing machine, catching a bus or driving a car – in other words, competencies central to the ability to cope with ordinary living. Most people not only acquire instrumental competencies as they grow older, but they become ever more sophisticated, possibly reaching a plateau in adult life.

Expressive needs may be understood as an emotional component of our psychological composition. In order for these needs to be met during childhood, a deep commitment is made between parents (or significant others) and their children. Therefore it is not sufficient for a child to mature with instrumental competency; he/she also has to experience the meeting of expressive needs. Examples of expressive needs are: friendship, a feeling of security, love and promotion of self-esteem. Therefore, a young adult should, after the formative years, emerge into an emotionally secure individual able to undertake everyday activities and to master the problems of everyday life.

Wolfensberger (1972) suggests that as a child grows and matures the role of parent is less concerned with transmitting and developing instrumental competence. This is because most children, as they grow, become more competent at meeting everyday challenging situations that they may encounter. However, the expressive needs remain and continue into adult life. These expressive needs, in adulthood, are usually met by, for example, an individual's spouse, children and friends.

Now that the meaning of instrumental competency and expressive needs has been outlined, it is appropriate to explain their centrality in understanding both the concept and subsequent practice of citizen advocacy. Consider the following scenario. A man with a mild learning disability, having recently moved to relatively independent accommodation in the community, experiences loneliness and isolation. It is highly likely that if this man were to need an advocate then the advocate's role would primarily be supportive, in other words, related to meeting his expressive needs. Another person with chronic mental health problems, with a history of self-neglect, might well require help and support in maintaining his/her instrumental competencies. In other words, the role of advocate is dictated by the need of the protégé rather than by having to conform to the provisions of particular caring agencies or professional groups. It is fair to say that these examples are simplistic and ignore, to some extent, the wholeness of human need. It is also important to remember that for Wolfensberger an advocate was not just a unidimensional concept, that is, friend, guardian or advocate. Rather, citizen advocacy is a complex concept that draws upon the many strengths of advocates to meet the many needs of the protégé.

Nurse and Advocate: Mutually Exclusive Concepts?

The author now considers the nurse as advocate and the attendant arguments both for and against, which support or deny the nurse's ability to act in this capacity.

Burnard and Chapman (1988) suggest that one of the responsibilities of the nurse is to act as advocate. They relate the difficulty patients experience in expressing their needs with that of the responsibility of the nurse to act as mediator in fulfilling these needs by speaking out for the patient. They qualify this by saying:

> The nurse who has truly cultivated the skill of empathy and who is in frequent personal interaction with the patient may be able to interpret the patient's needs to others and to act as a go-between when the other health care professionals appear, to the patient, to be unapproachable.

Indeed what is proposed here is clearly a component of a role that might realistically be undertaken by a nurse. However, whether this truly represents the role of advocate is problematic. This is because to act as go-between or interpreter would appear to fall short of many of the dimensions of the role of advocate.

Gadow (1983) argues for the practice of existential advocacy and believes that the nurse acting as advocate is the essence of nursing. She argues that self-determination is the most fundamental of human rights and that the nurse is obliged to act in the patient's interests, in the pursuit of such a right. She says that, in achieving such a right, it is up to the nurse and patient to determine the unique meaning of their interactions, so that the nurse can act as advocate in the pursuit of the patient's interests. However, she acknowledges that the nurse should not define these interests. The practice of the nurse acting as advocate should be based upon the principles of self-determination and holism. This, she suggests, can be achieved through the unique nature of the nurse/patient interaction. The dynamics of interaction, combined with an objective knowledge of the patient's condition and the pursuit of the patient's rights, represent existential advocacy. She summarises existential advocacy in three ways:

- The nurse assisting the individual in self-determination;
- The nurse giving of herself fully by her involvement with her patient;
- The nurse assisting the patient by understanding the patient's condition from an objective point of view.

MacIntyre (1983), on advocacy and nursing, asks to whom is the nurse responsible? In asking this, he identifies the need for a prior question, for what is the nurse responsible? He argues that a nurse's role is not functional in meeting patients' needs, rather is it concerned with acting as 'interpreter' for patients – someone who would act as mediator between the individual and the health care systems, in other words, an emissary between the cultures of the patient and the physician. Implicit in this role of interpreter is the need for the nurse to act as advocate for the patient.

Murphy (1983) identifies a model that he refers to as 'the patient advocate model of the nurse patient relationship'. Within this model the physicians' authority is seen as limited and the nurse is perceived to have equal status with them. Therefore, the nurse is seen as a significant contributor to the planning and implementation of care. This model identifies the nurse's obligations to respect the dignity and privacy of people. Perhaps even more significant is that the nurse is seen as accountable to the patient. The nurse in this model is seen as an enabler to facilitate the patient's movement towards self-actualisation.

Davis (1983) questions the nature of accountability because it appears to ignore the nurse's multiple loyalties and values. This brings the author to put forward arguments in contrast with those so far presented.

Wolfensberger (1983) believes that to represent the interests of another requires someone to undertake this role in a manner that minimises possible areas of conflict. He asserts this because he believes that, if there exists a conflict between an advocate's protégé and the interests of the advocate's employer or professional organisation, then the advocate is placed in an unenviable situation of choice, that is, a choice between the protégé's interests and those of the advocate. Wolfensberger considers that the outcome then will usually favour the interests of the employer or organisation at the expense of those of the patient. This is, perhaps, because most professionals give priority to the interests of their own organisation. This is one of the reasons why he asserts that the practice of advocacy cannot be undertaken by agencies or professionals. This is indeed problematic because much of the language used in relation to advocacy has been adopted by some professionals. In addition there is considerable nursing literature promoting the role of the nurse in advocacy. However, by acting as advocates, nurses may well experience conflict between their professional role and that of the role of advocate. This belief, concerning the considerable difficulties professionals face when adopting an advocate role, is based on, for example, career aspirations and at times mutually exclusive interests and loyalty. Perhaps this is why Wolfensberger (1983) identified a new scheme of advocacy for the protective services (those services in the United States of America caring for people with a learning disability) using citizen advocates. Williams (1989) suggests that non-professional advocates are much better placed to act in a representative role than nurses because of their relative freedom and independence. He is quite clear that this observation is not a criticism of nurses, rather a recognition of the very real differences between a professional service provider and an independent person. Williams (1989) describes seven components to the role of an advocate, these being:

- Speaking on behalf of a person or an issue;
- Representing that person or issue in a manner which will be perceived as if that person were the advocate's own;
- Pursuing the role of advocate with care and depth and feeling;
- Being prepared to invest more than could be reasonably expected from a professional;
- Being prepared to sacrifice elements of one's own life, for example, money, time and energy;
- Being prepared for hostility from those people who do not share an advocate's vision;
- Being prepared to put at risk one's job and one's health during the process of advocacy.

Activity 1.1

The reader is asked to reflect on these seven components, then set this book aside and jot down the name of someone for whom you have been caring recently and who may have needed some form of representation. If you had to speak for that person would you, if necessary, have been prepared to pursue the role of advocate in each of the components identified above? Where you feel unable to accept any of these, what is it about them that makes it difficult for you to act as advocate? How do you think your colleagues would react to your acting as advocate in all the seven components?

It is, perhaps, apparent that such commitments may place unrealistic demands upon the role of the nurse. Within nursing there would appear to be tacit rules governing the use of advocacy, that is, there are both written and unwritten expectations of a moral stance about nurses' everyday practice, and these expectations almost compel nurses to act as advocates. Therefore, there is perhaps a professional and morally-driven expectation, requiring a nurse to adopt an advocate role, regardless of the potential conflicts this may cause. An example of this moral code being an integral component of the nurse's role is examined by Thompson and Thompson (1985), who explore the process of ethical decision-making within nursing practice. They analyse ethical processes from a variety of philosophical paradigms. Kohlberg's (1981) moral development theory is used to facilitate understanding of ethical processes for decision-making. Within this theory it is suggested that moral development progresses through different levels of increasing complexity, the levels being sub-divided into different stages. A simplified description of these three levels is provided here to illustrate the sequence and universality of moral development:

Preconventional level. At this level it is suggested that children, up to the age of ten, do not use societal norms as a basis for moral behaviour. Rather, the standards used are based upon the authority of what others, for example parents, will do in response to their behaviour. Therefore the child has not yet developed his or her own belief system. Children then move to the conventional level of moral development.

Conventional level. At this level there is both adoption and maintenance of expectations of family, group and society rules. Indeed, it is the case that the rules of the group replace those of the parents as a source of authority which is no longer only expressed outwardly by reward and/or punishment. The child has now internalised a belief system that may be referred to as a conscience.

Principled morality. This final level is suggested to be reached in late adolescence. During this period of moral development there is a move beyond conventional morality. The level is characterised by two significant changes. The first of these is that the group used as a reference for rules and authority is one of which the young person is a full member. The second concerns the challenging and, if necessary, changing of rules, laws and/or regulations based upon clearly internalised principles. In Kohlberg's original writing he identified a further stage within level three, which was concerned with the universal ethical principle. Central to people reaching this stage was the belief that they must assume personal responsibility for their own actions, based upon universal and fundamental principles, an example of such a principle being the sacredness of life. Eventually, Kohlberg concluded that such a stage was purely theoretical and not grounded in empirical evidence.

★   ★   ★

These levels add a new dimension to the discussion so far, because if a nurse bases a moral decision on his or her stage of moral development, then the often-promoted moral obligation of a nurse's duty to act as advocate may not be as straightforward as some would like to believe. Despite this, there is a strong belief in the necessity for the nurse to act as advocate. Consider Beardshaw (1981) who says:

> The nurse's role as advocate is a logical extension of the resulting emphasis on patients' rights.

It is questioned whether there is an avoidance of the emotional and professional issues that may affect nurses should they adopt an advocate role. If a nurse acts out the role of advocate beyond some professionalised rearrangement of its concept, then this may result in problematic outcomes. These outcomes would be the direct result of pursuing advocacy beyond the boundaries of what might reasonably be expected of the nurse, that is, representing the interests of the patient without challenging the status quo of the organisation.

There is often an underplay or no acknowledgement of the potential negative outcomes related to the interplay of tensions between conflicts of loyalty that a nurse may experience. Beardshaw (1981) catalogues a whole range of malpractices, some of which are quite disturbing. She articulates the very real difficulties both students and practitioners of nursing face. Despite the grotesque nature of some of these affronts to people, she still promotes the, perhaps romantic, notion that nurses must act as advocates for their patients. Consider this example from her book, given by a student nurse:

> I have myself seen incidents of gross cruelty to geriatric patients by staff nurse, charge nurse, and nursing assistant on a ward I worked on, resulting in death. I was unable to report these incidents due to a lack of witnesses and a complete lack of faith in nursing management.

One could argue that nurses may unwittingly and naively find themselves in considerable difficulties whilst pursuing a 'holy crusade' of acting as advocates for their patients or clients. There is a very substantial difference between the role of an advocate and that of the nurse as professional practitioner. A nurse is expected to practise in an accountable manner, this being a requirement by both employers and the profession. Such a requirement means that, in the best interests of their patients, nurses do not operate as 'free agents'. This is in sharp contrast to citizen advocates, who, for example, are able to act with relative independence in order to safeguard the rights of their protégés.

For nurses, there are both ambiguities and difficulties related to the very real conflict of roles and loyalty. Tension between the roles of advocate and nurse may lead to conflict of loyalty between the nurse and the organisation for which he or she works. Beardshaw (1981) says:

> Loyalties and friendships within a hospital can be very
> close: nurses rely on each other when working. Making
> a complaint about a colleague can seem like betrayal.

This issue of loyalties and friendships is an interesting point that should be developed further. In some instances nurses could, perhaps, be accused of duplicity. Their own involvement in activities of which they would not wish others to be aware, may force them into containing certain situations in favour of the institutions' interests. A possible example of such duplicity is provided in one of the case histories later in this chapter.

This leads the author to pose the question, at what point in a caring relationship does the professional role of the nurse compromise the advocate role, or alternatively the role of advocate compromise the professional role? Consider the following case of Graham Pink, a charge nurse who worked for Stockport Health Authority. He had

spent some ten months attempting to bring to the attention
of his health authority the inadequate standards of care on
his ward. Following a letter he had published in the Guardian newspaper, he spoke publicly concerning inadequate
standards related to staffing levels. This was to lead to a
series of events in which he found himself suspended and
facing disciplinary charges concerning a breach of confi-
dentiality and failing to report an accident. Mr Pink,
despite the considerable media coverage of his plight, was
left in the main to the 'wolves':

> Management takes little note of nursing and if the
> profession allows me to be thrown to the wolves then it
> has only itself to blame if nursing's influence continues to
> decline.
>
> (Snell 1991a)

At this time the General Secretary of the Royal College
of Nursing stated:

> The punitive action taken against nurse Graham Pink . . .
> can only intimidate nurses everywhere from upholding
> the quality of patient care.
>
> (Snell 1991b)

To conclude this section, it is important to reaffirm that
nurses both can and should act as advocates on behalf of
their patients. This needs to be underlined, with the caveat
that many situations in which nurses may find themselves,
especially where there are tensions between patient, employer and/or a professional body, may place them in a
position of having to choose between their own interests
and those of their patients. There is no shortage of ideal-
istic, heady intellectual rhetoric within the nursing literature concerning advocacy, and there are few texts located
or grounded in the situations in which some nurses may
find themselves.

This section has presented to the reader wide-ranging

argument both supporting and rejecting the nurse acting as advocate. Also articulated is the importance and need to contextualise the adoption of such a role within some of the inherent problems that nurses may face.

Four Case Histories

This last section presents four case histories for the reader to reflect upon, each of which is authentic; however, names, locations, and some of the circumstances, have been amended to assure anonymity for the people involved in the histories. The reader is advised to share with colleagues his or her thinking on possible responses to the situations described, and is also asked to hypothesise the possible outcomes of any proposed action, including how other colleagues might react.

Possible questions to reflect upon might include:

Activity 1.2

To what lengths would you be prepared to go in acting as advocate for the patient?
How do you think you might deal with distrust, anger, sarcasm, obstructiveness from colleagues and managers?
Would you involve an independent advocate or would you attempt to resolve the incidents yourself?
Which form of advocacy would be the most appropriate for each of the situations?

It might help the reader to analyse the situations from the perspective of Wolfensberger's (1983) constructs of instrumental competency and expressive need.

Mr Dillon

Mr Dillon is 57 and recently approached his district nurse
at the local health centre concerning an impending appeal
tribunal against the Department of Health and Social
Security. He has been a frequent visitor to the health centre
over the last three years and he is well known. He is a
pleasant, kind man, married with three children, two of
whom are now grown up. He lives in a small rural community in a pleasant three–bedroomed council house, close
to the village pub. During his life Mr Dillon has held
several labouring jobs and is thought, by friends and
neighbours, to be a hard–working man. Whilst at the
health centre, Mr Dillon asked the district nurse for her
help. She remembered him from two years ago when she
visited his wife for a chronic health problem, and the nurse
agreed to listen to his difficulties to see if she could help
him. He explained that his Social Security office had
stopped his disability benefit because they felt he was able
to work, a point Mr Dillon adamantly denied. He told the
nurse that approximately one year previously he became
increasingly immobile due to osteoarthritis in his hands
and knees, and that, following diagnosis at the District
General Hospital, his General Practitioner, Dr Gold (a colleague of the nurse with whom she had worked for many
years), had 'signed him off' for six months. However,
when that certificate had run out, his Doctor seemed a
little reluctant to issue him a further certificate. Mr Dillon
explained that, two days after he had last seen Dr Gold,
Social Services wrote to him saying that his disability
benefit was being stopped and that he would have to claim
unemployment benefit. He informed the nurse that he
would have to attend a Tribunal and convince a panel that
he was still incapable of work. Towards the end of his story
he became tearful and told the nurse that he was unable to
support his wife and youngest child on unemployment

benefit, even with help from his grown-up children. At this point the nurse offered her help but explained that she had a house call to make, so they agreed to meet at Mr Dillon's house, with his wife, that evening. Later on that evening the nurse arrived at his house to see how she might help him. It became apparent, during their conversation, that there were other factors which Social Services might not have taken into account in deciding that Mr Dillon was not eligible for his disability benefit. He informed the nurse that approximately three years ago he suffered a cerebral haemorrhage resulting in epileptic seizures, for which he is currently taking medication. Besides this, he confides that he is unable to read or write, which is why he has always held labouring jobs. Evidently Mr Dillon's prospects of gaining employment would be negligible. He told the nurse that no one was able to help him. He has already approached Social Services for the help of a social worker, but they told him they had insufficient resources. He feels that his only hope, at a tribunal, would be to have someone represent him who understood his medical background and who would be able to persuade the tribunal panel that he was genuinely unable to work.

Julie

Julie is 28 years old, attractive, articulate and for at least some of the time is the type of person who wins many friends. However, Julie experiences extreme mood swings, fluctuating between periods of depression and periods when she appears almost manic. During a recent period of what her friends call 'being high', Julie's behaviour became so bizarre and unpredictable that her General Practitioner, in conjunction with her closest friend, persuaded her to be admitted to the local psychiatric unit as an informal patient. Rob, a mental health nurse, first met Julie two days after her admission. Since her admission she had been receiving oral medication, for which she had given her consent. Her general mood appeared euphoric, but it was pleasant, and Rob found himself liking her as a person. Over the next few days he spent much time with Julie as her named nurse. As time progressed it appeared that her mood became more stable and relaxed. However, Rob noticed a degree of antagonism between Julie and the charge nurse, Liam. He contemplated saying something to Liam but dismissed his observation as possibly due to his own over-sensitivity. Following some days off, Rob returned to the unit, and, during the hand-over period, was pleased to hear that Julie's mood had now been stabilised and that she had agreed to being discharged. Later Rob overheard Liam talking to one of the staff nurses about Julie, saying that 'his information would take care of that cocky cow'. That evening Julie returned to the unit in a very aggressive mood, shouting and swearing at the charge nurse. Rob attempted to calm her down by asking her what the problem was. She lashed out at him, stating that he must have known and that 'you and all the nurses are bastards'. She overturned a dining room table and threatened one of the other patients who attempted to stop her. She then stormed out of the unit in a very distressed state. Rob followed her for some time around the hospital grounds and eventually persuaded her to sit on a bench to talk to him. Still very angry and crying, she explained that Liam had told her boyfriend about her entire psychiatric history. She confided in Rob that she had been going out with a dentist for some time and that, when she was admitted to the unit, her closest friend had told her boyfriend that Julie had decided to go and stay with friends to think about his recent proposal of engagement to her. Julie also explained to Rob that she had confided in the staff nurse about her relationship, and the staff nurse, she is sure, told Liam. It emerged that Julie had gone to see her boyfriend that afternoon to say that she was ready to become engaged, but her boyfriend had told her that he had changed his mind. He also told her that he had been warned of her 'mental breakdowns'. Following a long period of talking and listening, Rob persuaded her to return to the unit. As they both returned to the unit they were met by the charge nurse, who was obviously angry with Rob for leaving the unit without his permission. He then told Julie that her behaviour on the unit was unacceptable and suggested that she leave the unit early. Without any warning, Julie launched herself at Liam, scratched his face, kicked him and called him a bastard. Rob and two other colleagues were forced into restraining her. The duty medical officer was called, who felt that she should be kept in the unit for a further period, on an emergency basis. The doctor prescribed a sedative to be given intramuscularly.

Richard

Richard lives in a community home for people with a learning disability. The extent of his learning disability is quite severe, but he is able to communicate verbally although his vocabulary is very limited. He manages to do most things for himself but there are a few self-help skills with which he requires assistance. Usually Richard is of a fairly quiet disposition, but is known to 'blow up' when one of the other two people living in the home interferes with anything in his room. The home is managed by a leader, deputy leader and four care officers. Margaret, a learning disability nurse, has worked at the home for a little over two years and, despite occasional tensions among the staff, she is very happy in her job as care officer. The officer in charge, Mary, runs the home smoothly and competently. When Margaret first came to work at the home she found it a little difficult to adjust to some of the working practices where she was afraid of being 'caught out'. These practices included finishing work early, occasionally using the residents' money to buy care staff drinks when on a visit to the local pub, and hiring out videos for the residents that only the care staff watched. However, over time, she grew to accept these practices as part of the job. Of all the practices, the most worrying to her was the way in which the deputy home leader, John, treated Richard when he occasionally 'blew up'. On one occasion she witnessed John manhandle Richard up the stairs of the home to his bedroom, in the process of which Richard slipped, sustaining considerable bruising and swelling to his forehead. At first she thought this was just an isolated incident, but during the first year of working at the home she witnessed several other incidents. Eventually she decided to confide in the home leader for her advice on what she should do. Mary explained to her that Richard could be very frustrating and difficult to handle. She also told Margaret that John was a very experienced person in the field of residential work for people with a learning disability. Margaret felt uneasy with her explanation and tried to press the point that this was not the correct way for a member of the care staff to behave. Mary explained that, perhaps, there were many things that the care staff did in the home, which were not exactly what the management of the service would accept as reasonable. She went on to point out that Margaret fitted in well at the home and enjoyed some of the 'perks', which she would not be able to do if the home were run in a very strict way. Margaret begrudgingly accepted this explanation. Some considerable time after Margaret's discussion with the home leader, a student nurse, pursuing a Project 2000 course, was sent to the home on placement. The student was allocated to work a shift that spanned both her own shift and that of the deputy home leader. The student soon settled into the life of the home and often commented on how much she was enjoying the placement. One afternoon the student approached Margaret and confided in her that she had witnessed an incident between Richard and the deputy home leader. She explained that, when Richard blew up because one of the other residents had been in his room interfering with his tapes, John had punched him in the abdomen. When Margaret asked the student whether she had said anything to the home leader, the student explained that she had not done so because she did not know how Mary might react. She went on to explain that she was thinking of reporting the incident to her personal tutor for his advice, but thought that she would approach Margaret first. Margaret's initial thought was to report the incident to Mary. However, when she reflected on her last meeting with her concerning this very issue, she remembered Mary's response. Margaret found herself in tremendous inner conflict on what to do. Reporting John officially might mean that she would be implicated in a number of incidents to do with petty theft, finishing work early and even misappropriating the residents' money. However, she now felt that, as the student nurse had brought this incident to her attention, she had no option but to support the student in discussing the incident with Mary.

James

Aeysha was pursuing a Project 2000 course, and during the common foundation programme she was required to undertake a child placement, which she had been looking forward to for some time. Just before she was due to undertake this placement her personal tutor asked to see her. He explained that there had been considerable difficulty in obtaining a children's experience placement for her. He explained that the college had negotiated a placement at a nursery. Her tutor informed Aeysha that, as the placement was new, it would be important for her to act as ambassador. She readily agreed to this and indicated that she would not let the college down, realising the need to act diplomatically. The first day of her placement came and she arrived at the nursery full of enthusiasm and determined both to enjoy and to learn from the experience. All the staff at the nursery were friendly and helpful, and identified opportunities to achieve her learning outcomes whilst on placement. She found interaction between the children and herself fun and stimulating. After her second week at the nursery, she noticed one of the little boys, James, to be a little reticent of all the nursery staff, as well as of herself. She mentioned this to one of the nursery workers, who dismissed it as possibly 'just a phase he was going through'. One morning James had an accident and wet his trousers. The nursery leader, Harry, asked Aeysha to take James to the changing room area to wash and change him into a spare pair of trousers. She took James to the changing area and undressed him ready for a wash. Whilst she was washing him, she noticed a series of bruises on his upper legs and abdomen. The bruises ranged in colour from dark blue to a yellowish brown. She also noticed what she thought to be bite marks on one of his buttocks. When she had finished washing and dressing him, she returned James to the play area and sought the immediate advice of the nursery leader. He took her to the staff room after she had explained that she had something urgent to tell him. She informed Harry of what she had seen. He was very sympathetic and thanked her for bringing her concerns to his attention. He explained that James' father had abused him physically and subsequently he had been removed from the family home by a court order. Aeysha pointed out that there were some bruises that appeared to be new, even though the bite marks looked old. Harry answered that many of the children had bumps, lumps and bruises, and that this was quite normal for children. He also told her that James had an older brother who was quite spiteful and was known to bite James when they 'scrapped'. Harry then explained that accusations against parents were dangerous if they were not handled properly. Aeysha found herself unable to accept this and told Harry that if he did not do something then she would!

The case histories provided identify situations which nurses do encounter. Readers can probably think of dilemmas that they have encountered where they have felt a need to act as a patient's advocate. Clearly, whether to act as advocate or not is not an easy decision. This issue is to be explored further in chapter 2.

Conclusion

In conclusion, some of the points thus far explored are highlighted. Firstly, it is important to restate that nurses can and should act as advocates in some circumstances. However, such a decision should be grounded in a full understanding of the possible consequences of enacting such a role. Nurses should not be made to feel guilty and obliged to act as advocates when, for either personal or professional reasons, to adopt the role would cause them distress. Rather, nurses should recognise the importance of an independent advocacy scheme, to which they are able to make a referral. Indeed, this ability to network services, external to the service in which they work, is a highly desirable skill of practitioners. Because of the possibly mutually exclusive role demands of nurse and advocate, it is, as stated earlier, inevitable that for a nurse to act as advocate may result in extreme tensions, some of which are identified in figure 1.1. This diagram depicts attributes of the roles of nurse and of advocate. In addition the diagram demonstrates the possibility of the two depicted roles being able to articulate. However, because

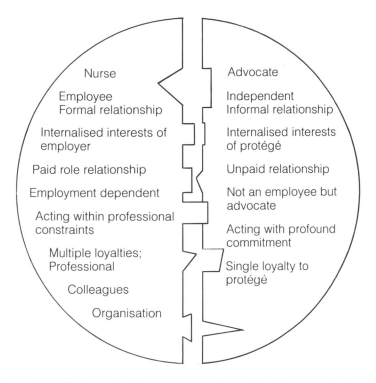

Nurse

Employee
Formal relationship

Internalised interests of
employer

Paid role relationship

Employment dependent

Acting within professional
constraints

Multiple loyalties;
Professional

Colleagues

Organisation

Advocate

Independent
Informal relationship

Internalised interests
of protégé

Unpaid relationship

Not an employee but
advocate

Acting with profound
commitment

Single loyalty to
protégé

Figure 1.1 The interface between role demands of nurse and advocate
demonstrating incumbent tensions and loyalties.

some of the role demands are mutually exclusive, it can be
seen that for a nurse to act in the role of advocate may not
always be possible, or even desirable. This is demonstrated
in the diagram by the internal edges of each half of the circle
depicting an interface that will not articulate.

   This chapter is intended to provide the basis for further
discussion and also the laying of a foundational, conceptual
framework for understanding advocacy in nursing. There
has been a deliberate attempt to draw from a wide variety
of texts and case histories. If the reader is interested in
pursuing particular areas of advocacy further, then the

references identified will provide far greater detail than is possible in this book.

In chapter 2, advocacy in context is described and discussed more fully. This will enable nurses to make professional judgements about whether to refer patients or clients to an independent advocacy service or to attempt to act as advocates themselves.

References

Bandman E (1983) Who will advocate for the nurse advocate? In Murphy C and Hunter H (eds) *Ethical Problems in the Nurse-Patient Relationship*. Boston: Allyn and Bacon.

Beardshaw V (1981) *Conscientious objectors at work: Mental hospital nurses: A case study*. London: Social Audit.

Burnard P and Chapman C (1988) *Professional and Ethical Issues in Nursing*. Chichester: John Wiley.

Butler K, Carr S and Sullivan F (1988) *Citizen advocacy: A powerful partnership*. London: National Citizen Advocacy.

Clarke L (1985) Rights and responsibilities and protection for people with mental handicap. In Sines D and Bicknell J (eds) *Caring for Mentally Handicapped People in the Community*. London: Harper and Row.

Davis A J (1983) Authority, autonomy, ethical decision making and collective bargaining in hospitals. In Murphy C and Hunter H (eds) *Ethical Problems in the Nurse-Patient Relationship*. Boston: Allyn and Bacon.

Dolan K and Taggart J (1972) How to get benefits for disabled adults. In Heron A and Myers M (1983) *Intellectual Impairment. The battle against handicap*. London: Academic Press.

Gadow S (1983) Existential advocacy: Philosophical foundation of nursing. In Murphy C and Hunter H (eds) *Ethical Problems in the Nurse-Patient Relationship*. Boston: Allyn and Bacon.

Gates B and Lewis D (1987) Learning to speak. *Senior Nurse*, **6** (2): 21–2.

Healy J (1983) Patients' rights and nursing. In Murphy C and Hunter H (eds) *Ethical Problems in the Nurse-Patient Relationship*. Boston: Allyn and Bacon.

Heron A and Myers M (1983) *Intellectual Impairment. The battle against handicap*. London: Academic Press.

Kohlberg L (1981) *Essays on moral development. Volume 1: The philosophy of moral development*. San Francisco: Harper and Row.

MacIntyre A (1983) To whom is the nurse responsible? In Murphy C and Hunter H (eds) *Ethical Problems in the Nurse-Patient Relationship*. Boston: Allyn and Bacon.

Murphy C P (1983) Models of the nurse–patient relationship. In Murphy C and Hunter H (eds) *Ethical Problems in the Nurse-Patient Relationship*. Boston: Allyn and Bacon.

Orgel G (1983) They have no right to know: the nurse and the terminally ill patient. In Murphy C and Hunter H (eds) *Ethical Problems in the Nurse-Patient Relationship*. Boston: Allyn and Bacon.

Sang B and O'Brien J (1984) *Advocacy: The UK and American Experiences*. Project paper No. 51. London: King Edward's Hospital Fund.

Snell J (1991a) Pink seeks allies after losing appeal. *Nursing Times*, **87** (29): 5.

Snell J (1991b) Union reaction. *Nursing Times*, **87** (29): 5.

Strong S (1992) Users in the driving seat. *Care Weekly*, 214: 9.

Sutcliffe J (1990) *Education of Choice and Empowerment*. National Institute of Adult Continuing Education. Milton Keynes: The Open University.

Thompson J E and Thompson H O (1985) *Bioethical Decision Making for Nurses*. Norwalk, Connecticut: Appleton-Century-Crofts.

United Cerebral Palsy Associations (1966) Proceedings of the conference on protective supervision and services for the handicapped, New Kensington, Pennsylvania, November 15–17. New York: United Cerebral Palsy Associations.

Webster Universal Dictionary (1975) New York: Harver Educational Services.

Williams P (1989) The value of Citizen Advocates. *Nursing*, **3** (44): 28–31.

Williams P and Shoultz B (1982) *We can Speak for Ourselves*. London: Souvenir Press.

Wolfensberger W (1972) *Citizen Advocacy for the Handicapped, Impaired and Disadvantaged: An overview*. Washington DC: The President's Committee on Mental Retardation.

Wolfensberger W (1983) *Reflections on the Status of Citizen Advocacy*. USA: National Institute of Mental Retardation.

CHAPTER 2

Advocacy in Context

In chapter 1 it was suggested that sometimes a nurse may need to refer her patient to an independent advocate or advocacy scheme. However, such a referral should only be made after a carefully thought out evaluation. The ability to discriminate between sound advocacy systems, as opposed to those which could prove harmful to a patient, either through lack of support or poor organisation, is important to a nurse practitioner. Therefore, before a nurse makes such a referral, it must be clear that it would be in her patient's interests.

The first part of this chapter provides the reader with a number of case histories of successful and unsuccessful advocacy projects. From the successful projects the author identifies those features that a nurse should look for before making a referral. The level of definition in describing these projects is from an organisational perspective, rather than an individual perspective, as was the case in chapter 1. The chapter then focuses on the experience of individual nurses acting as advocates and concludes by examining the multiplicity of contexts in which nurses work. This acknowledgement of contexts will be used to develop a 'trouble shooting' chart. The chart will demonstrate how nurses may best approach situations that may require them to act as advocates and will identify the inherent problems of acting in this way.

Unsuccessful Advocacy Schemes

Booth (1990) has reflected upon her experience of attempting to establish the Huddersfield Citizen Advocacy Group, which was set up for people with a learning disability. During the early stages of development the group applied for a grant to both Huddersfield Health Authority and Kirklees Social Services. Funding was sought for the full-time employment of a person to co-ordinate the activities of the scheme. In anticipation of their success and to promote the work of the group, they distributed two thousand leaflets widely to people in the Huddersfield area. Three months after their application was submitted, the group contacted Social Services to check on progress, and discovered that the application was still on the desk to which it had been delivered, where it remained unopened. Booth (1990) described a catalogue of disastrous outcomes related to this application – even the discovery that at one stage the Health Authority, despite continued reassurances, appeared to have lost the application form. Eventually the Health Authority turned the application down. Social Services requested a further application, but required one that would amount to half the original funding requested. At this stage the group had been some eight months in attempting to secure funding. Because of these difficulties, some members of the advocacy group left and joined other advocacy groups that had developed in the area. Eventually the original request for £45,000 funding was substantially reduced to £8,000 by Social Services.

Approximately one year from the initial application, the Huddersfield Citizen Advocacy Group contacted Social Services informing them that the group no longer wished to proceed with their application. Up to the date of publication of Booth's (1990) paper, some considerable time after the original request for funding, the group had received no official acknowledgement!

Booth (1990) identified a number of features, which she says are indicative of statutory bodies when they deal with voluntary organisations:

- Absence of written communication;
- Limited verbal contact by way of a telephone;
- Endless delays and prevarication;
- Contradictory messages;
- Poor liaison between and within both social services departments and the Health Authorities.

The reader is asked to reflect upon this example of an unsuccessful advocacy scheme. One must be careful not to make a quantum leap from the reading of one published paper, into believing that the author has presented all the salient 'facts' concerning an incident. There are always a number of perspectives from which we may try to understand the subjective experience of a situation. Clearly different people will interpret these experiences in different ways. This point is raised because it is important to view complex situations from as objective a stance as is possible. However, clearly the attempts of this group to develop an advocacy scheme were unsuccessful.

Activity 2.1

The reader is first asked to consider whether they would have referred their patient to this advocacy group?
Second, does the emergence of other advocacy groups indicate to the reader fundamental problems with this advocacy group?

Such questions are important to nurse practitioners. This is because they reflect legitimate concern by nurses to ensure the wellbeing of their patients by knowing that such an agency is competent to help.

Lindsay and Marler (1989) described a self-advocacy scheme in learning disability, membership of which originated from day as well as residential services. The group met fortnightly over a period of approximately two years and was involved in discussion and role play exercises. In short, the members were learning the skills of speaking up for themselves. A questionnaire was provided for all members of the group and their key workers to establish how successful the scheme had been. The reported results of the questionnaire revealed that group members were better able to cope with such things as being teased, ignored in shops, and refused service at public houses. The key workers indicated that group members appeared more willing to communicate. They also reported that in a minority of the members there appeared to be a reduction in egocentric behaviour, with a more considerate attitude being demonstrated towards others. The authors concluded that, despite progress made by individuals, the support given to them would not be comparable to help given by the general public, and this raises a fundamental question. The supposed payoff from any form of advocacy rests in the advancement or empowerment of the patient, client or protégé, and the scale of empowerment in this example is perhaps questionable. The authors suggest that society at large, perhaps, will not accept a changed image of learning disability. They also raise the question whether there is a danger of arousing in people with a learning disability expectations that cannot, or will not, be met. Although this example has been placed under the heading of unsuccessful schemes, both authors report that the self-advocacy group members had developed as people, wishing to be listened to and, in a sense, quietly demanding the same respect that all people are afforded.

More recently there has been a breakdown of an advocacy project in South Wales. This was established in 1988 (Marchant 1992) and evolved from the All-Wales Strategy (Welsh Office 1983) that articulated a need for advocacy schemes for people with a learning disability. The breakdown possibly occurred because of problems related to the scheme's lack of independence, there being close links with the South Glamorgan Social Services Department.

This close involvement of a statutory caring agency with an advocacy group is problematic, and the outcome of such a relationship clearly demonstrates the need for advocacy schemes to be independent of service delivery agencies. Indeed one member of the scheme stated:

> Is it an unreasonable assumption that South Glamorgan
> social services were threatened by the establishment of
> an effective consumer organisation for people it served,
> so they set it up to fail?
>
> (Marchant 1992)

Marchant (1992) identified a need for the management team of the scheme to acknowledge that improvements in the delivery of the service, from a service agency, should not be pursued through a citizen advocacy system.

Successful Advocacy Schemes

Having identified examples of advocacy systems that have been less than successful, it is important to account for some positive examples of advocacy. These examples are positive not only because of the establishment of successful advocacy groups and partnerships, but also because they have led to the advancement and empowerment of the client or patient.

Glasman (1991a) identified how the rights of psychiatric patients could be safeguarded by introducing advocates into hospital services. Early in the 1970s stories of ill-treatment and abuse of human rights were emerging from large psychiatric hospitals in Holland, and out of the reported appalling conditions emerged a new group called 'Clientbond'. This group developed from a group of parents who challenged a decision of managers at a children's psychiatric unit, which concerned the sacking of a psychiatrist. The 'Clientbond' gradually formed into

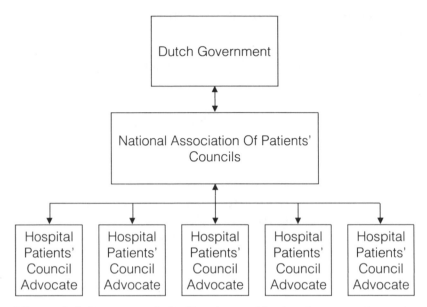

Figure 2.1 Structure of the Dutch psychiatric advocacy scheme in Psychiatric Hospitals.

advocacy groups within many of the psychiatric hospitals that became known as 'Patients' Councils'. In 1981 the National Association of Patients' Councils was formed to provide professional support to individual patients' councils throughout the country. The structure of the Dutch advocacy scheme is shown in figure 2.1.

The Dutch government agreed to provide funding for the foundation of a National Association of Patients' Councils. By 1982 eight advocates had been appointed and by 1991 there was only one hospital reported to be without an advocate. To promote the independence of the advocates an interesting dimension to the financial mechanisms was introduced. This involved hospitals paying the equivalent of each advocate's salary to the National Advocates Association, which then used this money to pay advocates in post. Glasman (1991a) suggested that, by ensuring that advocates were financially independent of the hospitals, this enabled a bonding trust to develop between the advocate and the client because the advocate was not reliant upon the hospital for financial stability. It should be noted that, whilst managers of the psychiatric hospitals in Holland are expected to listen to the councils, they are not necessarily obliged to put into force any of their recommendations. Perhaps this is why there are critics of the system, who claim that the power of the councils only extends to the decor of buildings and choice of foods on offer. Although Holland has enjoyed relative success with such an enlightened advocacy system, it is not without problems. In a subsequent paper, Glasman (1991b) identified that the democratic basis of the councils led to difficulties concerning the continuing use of electro-convulsive therapy (ECT). The councils attempted to communicate to hospital managers the variety of opinion concerning the continued use of ECT, but unfortunately this resulted in confusion, plurality of opinion and contra-dictory and diluted messages. A court ruling was eventu-ally obtained to the effect that the judiciary was not professionally competent to settle such an issue and left the use of such treatments to medical opinion. The outcome, despite the councils' attempt to prevent it, was the con-tinued use of ECT. A member of the 'Clientbond' stated that the various groups needed to work more closely together to ensure that common messages were sent to hospital managers to defend patients' rights. Even with these reservations, it appears that the scheme has attempted to provide a new and relatively independent advocacy scheme for people with mental health problems.

Another positive example of advocacy in action is a project recorded by Sang and O'Brien (1984). They pro-vided a detailed account of the development of the Advo-cacy Alliance group and a programme of befriending residents at Normansfield and St Ebba's, both large hospitals for people with learning disabilities. The authors identify three phases in the process of establishing this advocacy scheme.

1 The preparatory period

This first stage concentrated on developing realistic working agreements and relationships between Advocacy Alliance and two hospitals. A constituent charity of Advocacy Alliance, 'One to One', had already developed relationships with individuals within each of the hospitals. This paved the way for a stronger, more formal, relationship between the hospitals and the Alliance. It was agreed that Advocacy Alliance should undertake to raise the money necessary to finance the project. Time was then spent reaching agreement between the Alliance and the hospitals and identifying an ethical code for advocates, concerning relationships between advocates and the residents and staff of the hospitals. This code acknowledged staff tensions; however, it defended the primary role of an advocate that was concerned with representing and protecting the rights of the protégé. This code dealt with:

- the nature of the relationship between the advocate and the resident;
- the type of relationship between the advocate and care staff;
- the right of free access to the resident whom the advocate was befriending;
- the need for the advocate to attend to confidential issues;
- confirmation that the advocate should not take on work that could be seen as the role of a member of the hospital staff.

Besides this work, the Alliance sought the backing of local voluntary groups. These local groups already had established contacts and networks within the community that the scheme used positively in promoting the be-friending scheme. Therefore, local groups were used to support and promote the advocacy programme, rather than provide potential advocates.

2 Advocates: recruitment and selection

The second phase of the programme was concerned with recruiting and selecting prospective advocates. Firstly, a television appeal was made encouraging potential volunteers to come forward. The areas surrounding the hospitals were saturated with leaflets promoting the Alliance and the proposed advocacy scheme. The first tranche resulted in few advocates coming forward to support the scheme. This advertising campaign was subsequently followed by a second tranche that resulted in a larger number of advocates volunteering. Altogether some eighteen volunteers offered their services for the scheme. Each of the volunteers was then provided with intensive training encompassing a period of orientation that included:

- analysis of the role of advocate;
- analysis of the importance of loyalty to the resident;
- visits to the hospitals;
- the development of communication skills.

The training course extended over a period of three months, and afterwards time was taken to match advocates to the most appropriate residents.

3 Consolidation of the project

The third and last stage of the project was concerned with consolidating the project and identifying support that would be needed for the advocates. The major areas of support identified were:

Prejudice: It emerged that advocates could hold preju-
dicial attitudes towards people with a learning disability
and these needed to be addressed.

Life style: It became evident that advocates were used to
a non-institutional life style; therefore, having to build a
relationship with a person within the 'perverse' world of
an institution proved detrimental to the development of
relationships.

Withdrawal/Rejection: The development of a relationship with a vulnerable and non-valued person did not
always progress in the way that was expected by advocates. This was sometimes because of rejection by the
person with a learning disability. It became evident that
the advocates needed help in understanding rejection and
at times required emotional support.

Time: The role of advocate usually required an advocate
to give that which is most precious, 'time'. It became clear
that advocates needed to manage their time well and take
account of institutional routines.

Confidence: The demands upon advocates placed them
in situations where their self-confidence was constantly
taking knocks. Speaking up for someone, against possibly
authoritative figures, was not easy. This was especially so
when the commitment already developed by advocates
was lacking in authoritative figures in the hospitals.

This important contribution, by Advocacy Alliance, to
the development and promotion of advocacy created a
milestone in the acceptance of advocacy in institutions. Of
equal importance was the demonstration of the potential
for success of advocacy schemes independent of statutory
caring agencies.

The Camberwell citizen advocacy scheme was another

example of a successful project, especially concerning funding issues (Butler, Carr and Sullivan 1988). The Cambridge House Mental Handicap Project, established in 1978, resulted from an awareness that large numbers of people with a learning disability were not receiving any support from the statutory caring agencies. This concern was reinforced by the proposed closure of a large hospital in the locality (Darenth Park). By the end of 1983 the project became committed to people with a learning disability in the Camberwell area, with the establishment of a citizen advocacy scheme. The scheme attempted to secure funding from a variety of sources. These sources included the DHSS, the King's Fund, Sainsbury's, Cadbury's and the Home Office Voluntary Service Unit. Funding arrangements were difficult and complex. Because workers within the scheme carefully evaluated any condition of grant aid, the often-found problem of interference by sponsors did not prove troublesome. However, difficulty was experienced with the continuity of funding, that made forward planning difficult. With perseverance and a very committed staff, the Camberwell advocacy project is a success story, offering an advocacy service to the people of this local community.

Following this selective analysis of advocacy schemes from the literature, it is suggested that, before a nurse refers a patient to an advocacy scheme, the following issues should be carefully evaluated. These issues are firmly grounded in those factors that appear to have made some advocates and advocacy schemes successful. These include:

• Commitment;
• Good organisation;
• Independent funding;
• Effective communication.

The process of evaluating advocacy schemes and advocates is explored in far greater detail in chapter 5.

Agents of Change or Agents to be Changed?

The second part of this chapter explores the experience of carers, who by acting as advocates for their patients, have dared to challenge human service delivery agencies provided to people, within a variety of settings. The examples given relate to nurses who have spoken out for groups of people, rather than for individuals. A recent article by Young (1992) identified that nurses were becoming increasingly frightened to speak out for their patients, even when those patients were suffering. This was because many nurses were fearful for their future career. The article reported on a number of nurses who outlined their experience of 'speaking up' on behalf of patients. One nurse claimed to have lost her job after informing a senior nurse, in writing, of concerns related to the administration of medicines and under-staffing. Following the voicing of her concerns, a decision was made not to renew her contract and she was told to leave her position immediately. Before writing this letter, she had been praised for the quality of her work. Another nurse found that research data, related to Acquired Immune Deficiency Syndrome, were being falsified. When this was reported, the contract of this nurse failed to be renewed.

Smith (1980) offered a compelling paper that identified her experience in maternity care. Whilst holding the position of Director of Nursing in a county health department in the United States of America, a component of her role was to review statistical data concerning maternal and infant mortality and morbidity within the county. She became alarmed when the statistics showed a high level of episiotomies, perineal tears and low Apgar scores. The babies with low Apgar scores were born to women with no history of problems during pregnancy and uneventful labours, and she identified a high 10.3 per cent infection rate amongst the 559 mothers studied. This compared unfavourably with the 3.8 per cent infection rate found across the United States as a whole. Of the babies who had a low Apgar score, vacuum extraction was identified to be a significant factor in infant morbidity. She identified that this type of delivery was used for all the babies who had a low Apgar score. Following analysis of the data and literature search, she identified a need for further investigation. Her initial findings were presented to both doctors and nurses within the department. The response was one of indifference. However, a colleague continued to compile the data for a further three months and the results proved comparable to the original findings. Because of the significance of the findings, Smith (1980) attempted to introduce a systematic and more informative referral system in the maternity service. It was thought that this would improve communication between personnel within the hospital and, as a consequence, improve the care of both mother and baby. The data and concerns were again presented to colleagues, both medical and nursing. It is reported that senior administrators, doctors and nurses all indicated that the findings from the data were not worth pursuing. At one stage the colleague who had assisted with the second tranche of data collection was reported to have been told by a doctor 'not to worry her pretty little head with such matters'. Smith (1980) continued to confer with colleagues from a wide professional base. However, it became increasingly clear that nothing was going to be done to improve the situation. Frustration and discouragement arose from the fact that no changes were made for patients. This led her to make the decision to speak up as advocate for the patients. The response, perhaps, was inevitable:

> The result: the liaison nurse [the colleague referred to earlier] was denied further entry to the hospital, the hospital nurses were no longer allowed to give us any

information, and I resigned my position to retain my
principles and because I was told I was 'to be punished'.
I also paused and took stock: everyone had deserted me!
(Smith 1980)

It is almost inconceivable that one individual should
have to bear the burden of the responsibility of challenging
an entire organisational structure, and yet there is overwhelming evidence that such negativism is often the reaction to a nurse acting as advocate. Simply stated, all
this individual attempted to do was articulate her concerns
over what appeared to be unacceptable patterns of care.
To act in such a way is perhaps what would be expected
of all nurses in the interests of patient care. However,
the author would suggest that, although the position that
Smith (1980) took was laudable and clearly demonstrated
her courage, it was naive and misguided. It is for exactly
the reasons that she so clearly articulates in this example
that a nurse cannot on every occasion act as advocate. The
contexts that nurses work in and the complexities of those
contexts, coupled with the politics that occur within
organisations, make one individual, who already has multiple loyalties, an embarrassment and expendable to organisations.

There is clearly a need for advocates who are able to act
as change agents, to defend the rights and integrity of
people. Sometimes it may be necessary to challenge the
basis and quality of professional care, such as has been
identified in the previous example, although this brings
conflict for the nurse. If a nurse should adopt the role of
advocate, then this often means becoming an agent to be
changed rather than a change agent. Reflection upon the
contexts in which nurses work makes universal adoption
of an advocate role, by a nurse, at best unwise and at worst
possibly damaging to both the nurse and the patient. The
contexts in which nurses work have changed considerably

over the last few years. Consider some examples of change that have taken place within the Health Service in particular, as well as other important changes to Social policy legislation.

1. The National Health Service and Community Care Act, 1990.
2. Marketplace economy in the Health Service.
3. *The Patient's Charter* (DoH 1991).
4. The Children Act, 1989.

The principle of a nurse acting as advocate is not disputed. However, the differing contexts in which nurses work lead the author to conclude that a variety of approaches to enacting advocacy should be adopted, and that this should include nurses networking independent advocacy agencies. This chapter now considers those factors that make adopting the role of advocate potentially problematic for nurses. Also explored is a range of strategies, including networking, that nurses might wish to consider before deciding whether to adopt the role of advocate.

The Context in which Nurses Work

The chapter so far has outlined examples of the difficulties some nurses have experienced when acting as advocates. Nurses work within a variety of settings that are now explored and discussed. That nurses reflect deeply upon the settings in which they work is important. This is because understanding the context in which one works provides a reference point for rational decision-making on when it is appropriate, or not, to adopt the role of advocate. An important feature of the contexts in which nurses work is their plurality. Examples of these different settings include a busy surgical ward, community residential home, social education centre, elderly persons' home, National Health Service Trust, children's ward, community health team, acute psychiatric unit and even secure environments. Can it be that the practice of nursing and the incumbent role demands in each of these very different settings are the same? Can it be that customs, philosophies, ideologies, organisational values and norms in each of these settings are the same? In a community home for people with a learning disability, a positive and enlightened philosophy of care may be apparent. Care staff may be actively encouraged to pursue the rights of the individual because it is a supposed feature of enlightened ideology in learning disability. Alternatively, a nurse may work in an oppressive institutional environment, where people with a learning disability lead devalued lives. Such an environment may result in the rights of the individual being forsaken for the interests of the institution. These contexts lie at the extreme ends of a continuum that suggests that there is not even a single unifying ideology in one specialism of nursing, let alone in the differing settings in which nurses work.

Three types of environment, Supportive, Closed, and Hostile or Dangerous, have been identified by the author, evolving from a reflection of his practice as both nurse and independent advocate, rather than from any research studies. These environments or contexts are not necessarily institutionally dependent, that is, it is not only the setting which determines the context; attitudes of nurses towards patients, for example, are equally relevant. Therefore the term environment or context refers to a setting that could be a ward, a community home, a psychiatric unit or even a community-based setting.

Supportive environments

Within these environments there exists a warm and caring attitude towards patients. The environment is usually public in nature and, therefore, open to outside agencies and their personnel. There is a genuine desire to safeguard the rights of the individual. Care staff are encouraged to seek the help of an independent advocacy system in those cases where they are unable realistically to pursue or speak up for the rights of patients. Communication between staff is open, warm and friendly but remains professional. Multidisciplinary care is evidenced by different members of the care team collaboratively planning care. Morale is high and there is an overt cohesiveness that supports a positive ideology towards people.

Closed environments

By way of contrast to supportive environments, a closed environment is one where little interaction exists between the setting and external agencies. When interaction does occur with external agencies, it is guarded and defensive. Care staff work hard, but do not always demonstrate a deep concern for people. The completion of nursing tasks is seen as more important than the means by which completion of those tasks is achieved. The notion of an advocate entering the setting is frowned upon with scepticism. Where the role of advocate is tolerated, this is done so begrudgingly and with an overt disassociation from the advocate. Attempts by the advocate to work with her client are continually thwarted. There is an attempt to move towards multidisciplinary care. Morale in closed environments is usually high, but patients are not seen as integral components of that morale.

Hostile or dangerous environments

In complete contrast to both supportive and closed environments, there exist hostile or dangerous environments. Within these, there is little or no interaction between the setting and external agencies. Staff make no attempt to disguise their contempt for advocates or, as they are more often perceived, 'meddlers'. There is an 'unwritten law', within such contexts, of containment that forbids any member of caring staff to speak out for the patient. There is high cohesion between staff against another member of staff who dares to speak up on behalf of patients. Should someone speak up for a patient then they will be confronted with verbal aggression and/or intimidation. This may indeed be against the person as well as their property. Morale is stable, but only in that it maintains cohesion and protects collective culpability. Patients' or clients' rights do not feature as a high priority in nursing care. Rather, patients are seen as a homogeneous block of people requiring a homogeneous block of treatment. Multidisciplinary care is absent or carefully stage managed so that it appears to be present.

It is now appropriate to explore how nurses might react to situations requiring them to act as advocates. It is important for nurse practitioners to evaluate not just the situation that may require some form of advocacy, but also the context in which they work. This is because it is not simply a question of reacting to a given situation by deciding whether to act as advocate or not. A nurse should consider the variables of context of the situation encountered, and the type of advocacy or advocate that may be required.

Activity 2.2

The reader is asked to analyse critically each of the following three case histories and to decide, from the descriptions given above, the environment that is being depicted and also which type of advocacy, as detailed in chapter 1, is indicated for each situation. Using figure 2.2 as a guide to the relevant section, the reader should then consider the description of the probable outcomes of those decisions, which are given after the case histories. It must be remembered that any form of advocacy should be undertaken in full partnership with a patient: a nurse cannot impose advocacy upon a patient. Nurses must take into account the wishes, fears and aspirations of the people for whom they care. Wherever possible the reader is asked to discuss decisions concerning the case histories with colleagues or peers.

The Case Histories

The story of Flo

Nicki, a student nurse, had worked in a large district general hospital. The placement, care of the elderly, was an integral component of her chosen branch programme. She had found it difficult to get along with the staff, but she was happy to be 'lost' in her work by providing good patient care. Flo, an elderly woman, was admitted to the unit to stabilise her diabetes. After she had stayed on the ward for approximately three days, her consultant felt that she should be discharged. The qualified staff of the unit strongly supported this and the ward sister had actively encouraged the consultant to discharge her. During a visiting period Flo's son approached Nicki, saying that he was very concerned about what he perceived to be a very early discharge. Nicki directed him to the ward sister.

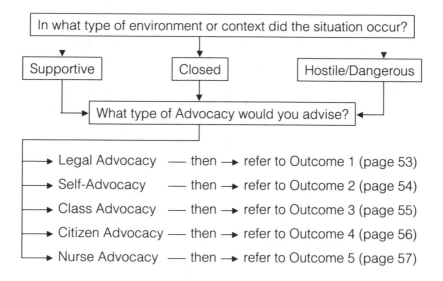

Figure 2.2 Flowchart of nursing contexts and possible advocacy approaches related to consequential outcomes of nurse decision-making.

Having spoken to the ward sister, he returned to see his mother and at the same time attracted Nicki's attention. He explained to her that his mother lived on her own and was becoming increasingly confused and unable to look after herself. He said that he was convinced that a district nurse had not been organised for her and that he was worried that she might wrongly inject herself with insulin or forget to administer it at all. His mother, he explained to Nicki, had no immediate family living nearby, and he lived some two hundred miles away. His mother then became very tearful, telling Nicki that she was confused about her future. She pleaded with Nicki to help her by explaining to the sister that she should not be discharged until they (the consultant and qualified nursing staff) were sure she would be able to cope.

The story of Henry

David had been allocated to a continuing care facility for
people with long-standing mental health problems. This
unit, in the suburbs of a large industrial town in the North
of England, had been developed because of the closure of
a large Mental Illness Hospital. The unit was staffed by
qualified and unqualified nurses and other therapists who
provided twenty-four hour care. There were approximately thirty people who lived at the unit, organised into
three care groups. Each of the care groups occupied a
different part of a substantial Victorian building. The
underlying philosophy of this arrangement was to encourage personalised small group care. When David arrived at
the unit he found that he was working with a nursing
assistant for much of the morning in 'Red group'. One of
the first things he noticed about the home was a rather
unpleasant smell that, he was told by the nursing assistant,
was caused by Henry's incontinence. Despite the relatively
recent work to the building, it looked dirty and uncared-
for. David did his best to get to know both the people of
the care group and the nursing assistant. He asked the
nurse numerous questions about the unit, the people who
lived there, and the different types of health care workers
who were employed in the unit. All of his questions were
met with indifference or with comments such as 'I don't
know' or 'I only work here'. Having made little progress
in finding information about the unit, he decided to wait
for other nursing staff who were on duty later that day.
During the morning he developed a rapport with the
gentleman called Henry, who informed David that there
was little in the home to do. Later on that day the staff
nurse arrived for the afternoon shift. She was intrigued by
David's course and was especially interested in the idea of
a Diploma, as this would help her in her career. Unfortunately David's questions concerning the unit were met

with the same indifference as in the morning. He also
noted that a hand-over had not taken place when the staff
nurse arrived for duty. Over the next few weeks David's
relationship with Henry developed and one afternoon,
when they were left alone, Henry told David of his misery.
He pleaded with David to get him out of the unit, saying
that he was happier at 'that bin on the hill'. He complained
that he never saw anyone and had twice tried refusing his
tablets, but was always told that he must take them. He
complained that when the staff became bored they took
it out on the patients by teasing and sometimes physically
abusing them. He begged David to help him stand up to
the nurses and find him somewhere else to live. David
had one week left on placement at the unit!

The story of Sally

Sally, a four-year-old toddler with Down's syndrome,
spent most of her time living at home with her mother,
father and two older brothers. She attended an ordinary
play school as her mother and father were keen for Sally
to experience the same opportunities as other children of
the same age. In support of the family, the parents were
offered periods of respite care from a local residential home
for children with a learning disability. When Sally's
parents had explored the possibility of her attending an
ordinary primary school, the Local Education Authority
had indicated that they felt Sally's needs would be better
met in a special school. This brief history was explained
to Denise, a newly qualified nurse, by the community
learning disability nurse on the way to visit the family. The
community nurse visited the home on a frequent basis,
providing a point of contact and support for the family.
The relationship between the community nurse and the
family appeared very positive. During this visit to the
home Denise was involved in a discussion with the parents

concerning what the community nurse could offer to enable Sally to attend an ordinary school, just like all her friends. The parents accepted that Sally was a very slow learner, but insisted that she would be able to contribute to the life of the school in a positive way. They also explained that her nursery teachers were keen to support them in trying to get Sally into an ordinary school. Both parents indicated that they would like the community nurse to help them by advising them what to do and speaking up for them against what they described as the 'mindless bureaucracy' of the Education officials. The community nurse explained that she was not sure that she would be able to help and that she would need to consult with other colleagues. The parents and the nurse agreed a date to discuss options open to them and at which she would be able to advise them how she would best be able to help them. The community nurse and Denise left the house to return to the offices of the Community Learning Disability Team, and when they returned to base the nurse explained to Denise that she did not want to get involved!

The Outcomes

Outcome 1. Using legal advocacy in:

a) **Supportive Environments:** Legal Advocacy is seldom required in supportive contexts. Often carers are encouraged to enable patients to overcome their difficulties. However, sometimes this type of advocacy is required for detailed and complex legal work in support of, for example, Tribunals, protection orders or guardianship orders for children. If this was the reader's response in this environment they would be supported in recommending this type of advocacy.

b) **Closed Environments:** As this type of environment is relatively detached from external agencies, a nurse would find great difficulty in obtaining peer support for suggesting the use of a legal advocate. However, colleagues in this environment would have to co-operate, albeit reluctantly, with an external advocate. The use of a legal advocate would enable patients to safeguard their rights through appropriate representation.

c) **Hostile/Dangerous Environments:** It may be that in such an environment this type of advocacy, with the power of legislation, may be the most effective in securing the rights of an individual, whilst at the same time empowering that person.

Outcome 2. Promoting self-advocacy in:

a) **Supportive Environments:** Almost all supportive environments would actively encourage self-advocacy. Belief in the empowerment of people enables carers to feel secure in encouraging patients or residents to speak up for themselves. A nurse will receive encouragement and support from peers in promoting this type of advocacy. The act of self-advocacy and the enabling of that act, by a nurse, are highly valued in this type of environment.

b) **Closed Environments:** Any attempt by a nurse to encourage patients to speak up for themselves will be met with resistance. Patients are seen as passive recipients of care with no right to question elements of that care. Nurses should think about, and advise their patients of, alternative forms of advocacy in this type of environment.

c) **Hostile/Dangerous Environments:** Of all the different types of advocacy and contexts in which advocacy could be practised, self-advocacy in a hostile or dangerous environment is virtually impossible. Such an environment does not believe in the empowerment of people. Patients are perceived as mere objects to be tolerated during the working day. A nurse practitioner must never encourage her patients to speak up for themselves in this type of environment and should seek an alternative form of advocacy as a matter of urgency.

Outcome 3. Seeking the support of class or collective advocacy in:

a) **Supportive Environments:** The reader will remember that class or collective advocacy is concerned with representing the interests of specific segments of society, for example, Age Concern, MIND and MENCAP. These are ideal organisations to which nurses may recommend their patients. Supportive environments often make available leaflets and information on such organisations for patients. If a nurse is unsure how best to help someone, this form of advocacy, in this type of environment, is ideal.

b) **Closed Environments:** Closed environments do not interact or articulate well with external agencies. Members of staff working in closed environments are extremely suspicious and unhelpful to any external agency. This is especially so if they perceive either the agency or individual advocate as being more knowledgeable of the problems affecting the patient. However, given that in this context it would be difficult for a nurse to act as advocate, the choice of class or collective advocacy is a sound one. A nurse should recommend this form of advocacy to a patient tactfully, to avoid possible conflict between herself and colleagues.

c) **Hostile/Dangerous Environments:** As in closed environments, these environments do not interact well with external agencies. However, because of the specialist level of skill and the resources such groups have at their disposal, class or collective advocacy would be an ideal choice. In some circumstances, in mental health for example, not only are such agencies able to provide advocacy but they can also provide access to information from a team of regional or national specialists. However, referral of your patient to collective or class advocacy should be undertaken carefully; this will protect the patient as well as the nurse.

Outcome 4. Seeking a citizen advocate in:

a) **Supportive Environments:** As with other types of advocacy in supportive environments this would be an ideal choice. The strong element of a partnership and the befriending nature of that partnership would be welcomed by carers. A nurse could facilitate a referral to a citizen advocacy system by attempting to identify the nature of need, that is, instrumental or expressive.

b) **Closed Environments:** Within a closed environment, a citizen advocate can be an ideal partner and friend for any patient. However, this environment would not welcome the advocate. The advocate would be treated with suspicion and would seldom receive any cooperation. Therefore, it would be important for a nurse to refer the patient to an advocacy organisation where there is adequate training and support. Clearly, in an environment where it is difficult to pursue the rights of an individual, this would be an ideal response from a nurse.

c) **Hostile/Dangerous Environments:** This type of environment makes it extremely difficult for a nurse to act out any form of advocacy role. Because of the almost oppressive nature of care and the devaluing of people being cared for, citizen advocacy is probably the most appropriate form of advocacy for this environment. Clearly, if there are legal implications, they need to be taken into consideration by the nurse. In this type of environment patients often desperately need both befriending and a partner. A referral by a nurse should be made as quickly as possible, in collaboration with the patient. As with other forms of advocacy, in this type of environment great care should be taken to protect the patient.

Outcome 5. Acting as a nurse advocate in:

a) **Supportive Environments:** Within a supportive environment a nurse will be encouraged to represent the rights and interests of his or her patients and to value the patient as a person. Because of the effective communication skills, multidisciplinary practice and high morale, the practice of nurse as advocate is embraced as an integral component of nursing care. Should nurses respond to a particular situation by acting as advocates then they will be supported and valued by their peers.

b) **Closed Environments:** Within a closed environment it is unlikely that colleagues would support a nurse acting as advocate for his or her patient. The nurse would be perceived as a threat to the integrity of the detached nature of nursing care practised. The nurse would probably cease to be a member of the 'gang', and, if such nurses persisted in acting as advocates for their patients, would suffer a peer response which would range from sarcasm to being ostracised by colleagues. Nurses would be advised to choose another form of advocacy in this context.

c) **Hostile/Dangerous Environments:** To respond, in a hostile environment, as a nurse advocate is extremely dangerous. Clearly in such environments a nurse would be well advised to use known networks external to the environment in which the nurse is working, to seek an independent advocate or advocacy system. The response of not acting as advocate for a patient may well result in feelings of guilt and anxiety on the part of the nurse. There may well be a need for the nurse to discuss this with a trusted colleague. Referral by a nurse to an independent advocate needs to be discreet and the patient needs to be made aware of possible alternatives.

Conclusion

In this chapter, examples of successful and unsuccessful advocacy projects have been outlined. The study of and reflection upon such projects are important because, if nurses are to be able to advise patients as to an appropriate advocacy system, they need to be able to identify those features that make the systems successful. The concept 'agents of change or agents to be changed' has been introduced, and types of environment described in a way that may help nurses to formulate decisions whether to act as advocate or to network other agencies. Decisions that a nurse makes concerning advocacy will inevitably result in both expected and unexpected consequences, which may include threats to their continued employment and practice as a nurse. Also, there are very real and complex emotional effects that nurses may experience should they choose to act as advocates (Copp 1986).

Finally, it is questionable whether a nurse is able, or indeed is the most appropriate person, to act as advocate. Few writers in nursing literature appear to articulate this concern, notable exceptions being Castledine (1981), Allmark and Klarzynski (1992) and Mackay (1993). Chapter 3 will further explore advocacy and nursing and will include discussion of the ways in which the practice of advocacy affects the role of the nurse from a personal and professional perspective.

References

Allmark P and Klarzynski R (1992) The case against nurse advocacy. *British Journal of Nursing*, **2** (1): 33–6.
Booth W (1990) Dependent, frustrated and devalued. *Community Care*, 844, 13th December: 23–5.
Butler K, Carr S, and Sullivan F (1988) *Citizen Advocacy: A*

powerful partnership. London: National Citizen Advocacy.

Castledine G (1981) The nurse as the patient's advocate: Pros and Cons. *Nursing Mirror*, **15** (20): 38–40.

The Children Act 1989. London: HMSO.

Copp L A (1986) The nurse as advocate for vulnerable persons. *Journal of Advanced Nursing*, **11** (3): 255–63.

DoH (1991) *The Patient's Charter*. London: HMSO.

Glasman D (1991a) The challenge of patient power. *The Health Service Journal*, 101, 5th September: 16–17.

Glasman D (1991b) Divided Opinions. *The Health Service Journal*, 101, 12th September: 20.

Lindsay A and Marler R (1989) Unrealistic expectations? *Nursing Times*, **85** (42): 33–4.

Mackay L (1993) *Conflicts in Care: Medicine and Nursing*. London: Chapman & Hall.

Marchant C (1992) Advocacy project failed under SSD influence. *Community Care*, 913, 30th April: 4.

The National Health Service and Community Care Act 1990. London: HMSO.

Sang B and O'Brien J (1984) *Advocacy: The UK and American Experiences*. Project paper No. 51. 9–26. London: King Edward's Hospital Fund.

Smith C (1980) Outrageous or outraged: a nurse advocate story. *Nursing Outlook*, 28, October: 624–5.

Welsh Office (1983) All-Wales strategy for the development of services for mentally handicapped people. London: HMSO.

Young S (1992) Nurses fear to speak out as patients suffer. *Sunday Observer*, 19th April: 7.

CHAPTER 3

Role and Advocacy

This chapter develops and expands upon the issues, out-lined in chapter 1, concerning the strains and stresses associated with enacting the roles of nurse and advocate simultaneously. Further exploration of this area makes necessary the consideration of a theoretical perspective of role applied to the practice of nursing. This chapter also explores some of the consequences nurses may experience should they act as advocates, consequences which pose threats to the health of the nurse and perhaps demonstrate why some nurses are either reluctant to act as advocate, or choose to recognise advocacy as a component of their role only when speaking up is unavoidable (Mackay 1993). This means that some nurses will speak up for patients only when the public nature of the situation, or the severity of the problem, leaves the nurse little choice – a very different matter from a nurse acting as a true advocate for a patient, which should be dependent on need, rather than on a nurse's fear of retribution. The final section of this chapter describes an alternative approach to the way in which nurses could learn about the theory and practice of advocacy. It is proposed that current approaches to the teaching of advocacy to the novices of the profession per-petuate a status quo, one that strengthens the profession's control and containment of nurse practitioners who wish to speak out for their patient or client, but are fearful of the consequences.

Role

Role has been defined in a number of ways. Often definitions are governed by the different theories that explain this phenomenon from a sociological perspective. One definition that facilitates our understanding of the concept of role is offered by Conway (1988) who says 'Role has its roots in theatrical usage, and refers to a part one plays or is assigned in a drama'. This definition belongs to the theoretical perspective known as **functionalism** that is attributable to Parsons (1951) and Durkheim (1964). Conway (1988) identified a number of central features attributable to the functional perspective.

Attributes of the functional perspective of role.
External objects and persons are seen as stimuli that act on an individual.
The action of an individual is a response to the norms and demands of a situation.
Behaviour is scripted with little interpretation of actions, individuals merely respond to one another.
Persons act on the basis of learned responses.
Groups act as an expression of societal demands and a shared system of social values.

It can be seen that functionalism reinforces the dramatic nature of role enactment and suggests that actors follow carefully crafted scripts. These scripts support the character credibility of an actor in portraying an 'assumed' role. It is proposed that the roles people adopt, within all contexts of life, are learnt through a process of **socialisation**. Elkin and Handel (1972) use the term socialisation to refer to 'The process by which someone learns the ways of a given society or social group so that he can function within it'.

Therefore, nurses are socialised into the role of nurse in just the same ways as they are socialised into other significant roles, for example son, daughter, father and mother. It is important that the novices of nursing learn the expected behaviours of the nurse which, when enacted, provide an outward expression of adopting and acting out the role. There are a number of studies that have catalogued the professional socialisation of nurses and other disciplines (Becker 1963; Melia 1987). Social psychology would appear to support the view that socialisation is not a passive process, but one in which the recipient is gradually 'brainwashed' through an organisation cloning exercise. However, Melia (1987), Mackay (1993) and others suggest that the process of socialisation will make heavy demands on a nurse who attempts to undertake the role of advocate.

When the demands of one role conflict with those of another then a nurse practitioner may experience **role conflict**. Role conflict is defined by Spencer (1979) as 'the situation in which a person occupies two roles that are regulated by incompatible norms', and by Hardy (1988), who says 'Role conflict is a condition in which existing role expectations are contradictory or mutually exclusive'.

A role occupant will experience psychological discomfort when the demands of two roles are incompatible, and this will manifest itself in a number of different ways. Firstly in intra-role conflict there is conflict with the demands others make upon the individual; for example, students of nursing may experience difficulty when their teacher encourages them to speak up for their patients, whilst their clinical colleagues do not. Alternatively a role incumbent may experience inter-role conflict, where there is conflict between the demands of one or more roles that an occupant may have adopted. An example of this may be a nurse attempting to act as advocate and nurse simultaneously. Should role conflict continue without some form of resolution, the role occupant will inevitably experience role strain. Role strain refers to a state of anxiety, tension, frustration, apathy and futility. Clearly this is an unhealthy condition for a practising nurse to be in and must be avoided at all costs. Apart from the functional perspective of role discussed in this section there are other perspectives that the reader may wish to pursue within the area of role theory; a suggested text is *Role Theory: Perspectives for health professionals* by Mary Conway and Margaret Hardy (1988).

Nonetheless the functional perspective of role does provide an excellent framework for a discussion on the role of nurse and advocate. Throughout this book, the reader has been encouraged to question whether there are distinctive differences between the role attributes of nurse and advocate; the next section attempts to further this discussion.

Activity 3.1

The reader is invited to list the major attributes of their role and then identify those that would cause conflict if the reader were to adopt the role of advocate.

Nurses, Professionalism and Advocacy: A Critical Argument

The role of the nurse has been defined by a large number of nurse theorists, for example Meleis (1988). There is a view that the many definitions offered fail to incorporate the significant role attributes of a nurse into a universal definition that is acceptable to the wider audience of nurse practitioners. This is probably because nursing is a large profession, where there is heterogeneity of professional background, context of work and ethos of practice. This, not surprisingly, has led to a multiplicity of theoretical explanations of nursing. For the purposes of the following discussion it is assumed that nursing refers to a generic practitioner who cares for people in a generic context and ethos. Henderson (1966) defines nursing as:

> The unique function of the nurse is to assist the individual, sick or well, in the performance of those activities contributing to health or its recovery (or to peaceful death) that he would perform unaided if he had the necessary strength, will or knowledge. And to do this in such a way as to help him gain independence as rapidly as possible.

Using this definition, the reader is asked to reflect upon the diagram that was developed in chapter 1. In figure 3.1 it can be seen that the roles of nurse and of advocate do not articulate. In addition, it has already been suggested that the attributes of the two roles may at times be mutually exclusive. There are potential tensions that exist between the offered definition of nursing and the operationalised practice of nursing and advocacy as detailed in figure 3.1. This is because it is only in the context of practice that the adequacy of a definition of nursing can be evaluated. Clearly, it is possible for definitions to exist as theoretical abstractions; however, these do little to promote an understanding of the nature of nursing, either at the universal level or at the health care interface. Henderson (1966) states that the function of the nurse is to assist an individual, regardless of whether that person is sick or well, in performing activities that contribute to health or its recovery. This, as a facet of caring, would be difficult to dismiss. However, what is meant by 'well' and what is meant by 'contributing to health or its recovery'?

Consider a patient or client, in this instance a child in a hospital ward, who is apparently being 'bullied' by nurse A, a nurse 'booked in' to cover for staff absences. The child is unhappy, in tears and obviously upset, and complains to nurse B that nurse A frightens him. Nurse B speaks to nurse A who tells her that she (nurse B) is too involved and not sufficiently objective in her care of the children. Being dissatisfied, nurse B complains to the ward sister, who reminds her that the ward is short staffed, which is why nurse A has been booked in. Now, is nurse A contributing to the recovery of health for this child? The author would argue, and hopes the reader would too, that this is not the case. Therefore, in order for nurse B to contribute to the promotion of the recovery of health for this child, she may well feel a need to speak up for him, to act as his advocate. Herein lies a tremendous tension between the definition of nursing offered, on the one hand, and the role demands of the nurse on the other.

Figure 3.1 identifies six demands that make advocacy difficult, at the very least, for nurses. Firstly, there is the issue of being an employee and the expectation of maintaining the 'nurse–patient relationship'. Secondly, because a nurse may possibly have worked within the organisation for a number of years she cannot hope to have avoided internalising the interests of the organisation. Her employment is dependent upon doing 'essentially' what is reasonably expected of her and therefore her livelihood is dependent upon her employment. In the example above, the child will soon leave the hospital, and the reader is asked to question whether the experience will have interfered with his recovery of health. It should also be remembered that the nurse, unlike the child, will not be leaving the organisation; she still has to work with a range of personnel from a range of disciplines, who may have been implicated should the nurse have acted as advocate for the child.

Collectively, the role demands of the nurse identified in figure 3.1 make the practical application of the offered definition of nursing problematic. Castledine (1981)

Figure 3.1 The interface between role demands of nurse and advocate demonstrating incumbent tensions and loyalties.

identifies a number of factors that make the nurse an inappropriate advocate:

- The nurse's unique role results in the patient being forced to be dependent on her for fear of pain and suffering;
- The general educational background is inadequate;
- The patient has little choice of who is to act as his advocate; and
- Even if the nurse does act as advocate for the patient she/he may not be able to do this independently from

the constraints of the institution or authority of the employer.

Allmark and Klarzynski (1992) draw a satirical analogy between the nurse acting as advocate and a policeman acting as advocate for someone in his custody; it is quite clear that a policeman may not be the most appropriate person to do this!

Emotional Consequences of Acting as Advocate

Throughout their career, it is almost inevitable that nurses will encounter situations that will deeply trouble their consciences. An excellent text that deals with this area is provided by Clay (1987). He offers realistic and pragmatic discussion on dilemmas of conscience and relates them, in part, to the practice of advocacy. A significant component of such dilemmas for nurse practitioners is the emotional consequences that they invariably bring. Developing relationships – sometimes strong – with people can, when put in the context of a sustained caring relationship, lead to emotional involvement. Abel-Smith (1987) notes: 'Exposed to human contacts of this kind [here he refers to close patient contact], the risk of emotional involvement becomes the greater with the consequential psychological stress'.

Such emotional involvement, coupled with circumstances in which a nurse must stand up and speak up for her patient, may well lead to stress. This is because the commitment to the emotional involvement, plus the necessity to respond to professional demands, may well bring about a dilemma of conscience. There would appear to be a need to reconcile such dilemmas; that is, there needs to be a reconciliation between the personal and professional demands made upon the nurse.

Nurses may encounter a range of emotional consequences when attempting to act out the role of advocate.
Some of these consequences may be the direct result of a
failure to bring about a reconciliation between the tensions
previously described. Some suggestions are offered as to
how nurses may manage such consequential feelings in
order to maintain their own health. The emotional consequences discussed are illustrative; they are intended to
reinforce the contention that, for nurses, advocacy is a
serious business with obvious and potentially threatening
consequences to their health. Copp (1986) states that
'Advocacy is not a slogan or a hobby nor is it to be entered
into by the faint hearted'.

Copp (1986) also identifies the concept of feeling the
'heat'. This she describes as when a nurse is caught in the
middle of complex social interactions that usually include
highly charged emotional exchanges. Such a formula has
the potential to excite 'chemical' reactions of such a magni-
tude as to cause ill health to the nurse.

Guilt

Guilt may be understood from two perspectives. The first
is an individual perspective, when, for example, a nurse
acts as advocate for an individual against a known individual practitioner. The second is an organisational perspective, when a nurse acts as advocate for an individual
against an organisation. Concerning the former, the
author has occasionally, but not very often, known a professional to be reproached about some aspect of his or her
professional practice following the intervention of a nurse
advocate. Reporting a colleague can lead to feelings of
guilt, even when it is quite clear that the other professional
was in the wrong.

Consider the following account of a nurse who spoke up
for a patient when she accused another nurse of physically

assaulting a young woman with a severe learning disability. Following a series of events involving the nurse advocate, the other nurse and members of the hospital management committee, it was agreed that the alleged incident took place and that some form of action would be taken against the nurse who had assaulted the young woman. The form of action taken was that the nurse was removed from the ward where she was working to another and she also received a written warning that such conduct, if repeated, would lead to her dismissal. However, the issue of the nurse being moved from her ward was not as straightforward as might be expected. This nurse worked in a ward where there was an extra payment made because of the challenging behaviour of the people who lived there. This enhanced payment was lost to the nurse when she had to move wards. The financial impact this had upon the nurse's family was significant. Would the reader handle this situation in the same way?

When you act as an advocate, or seek the services of an independent advocacy scheme, it will often mean that colleagues or the organisation for which you work will have to be 'reported' in some way. This has now become popularly known as **whistle blowing**. The author does not equate advocacy and whistle blowing. Rather, whistle blowing should be accounted more accurately in literature as a form of public advocacy, usually undertaken when all attempts at local resolution have been exhausted. The action of reporting one's colleagues often leaves nurses feeling ashamed in some way. The implicit trust that exists between nurse colleagues has to be forsaken in order for them to pursue something they believe to be right. It is easy to say that nurses have no need to feel ashamed, but such a sentiment seldom reduces the turmoil experienced by a nurse who has chosen to act as advocate. It is important to air such feelings to a friend or an independent counsellor. It is also imperative that nurses view their actions and the consequential outcomes in perspective and as objectively as possible. 'Self-flagellation' by a nurse advocate seldom resolves difficulties, especially of a psychological nature. Although people do sometimes triumph over organisations and natural justice does sometimes prevail, organisational fortresses are often impervious to the actions of an individual advocate. It should be remembered that, if nurse practitioners choose to act as advocate for their patient or client, feelings of guilt may be something that they have to come to terms with.

Fear

Fear may be defined as an 'Emotion, state of mind, caused by a sense of impending danger, misfortune, pain, terror, dread' (Webster Universal Dictionary 1975).

There is evidence of fear originating from physical and psychological sources being associated with the nurse acting as advocate. The literature (see chapter 2) would appear to suggest that the commonest cause of fear in the nurse advocate is that of threat. Reference can be made, for example, to continuity of employment, contractual arrangements, movement from the existing place to another place of work, and also of being 'sent to Coventry'. Threats may be even more sinister. Prior to the recent inquiry at Ashworth Hospital (HMSO 1992) a psychologist received a note from within the hospital that stated that she 'would get a fatal stabbing' (Lloyd 1992). The note appeared to have been sent to her as a result of her attempts to have National Front posters removed from the walls of the hospital. Crude but nonetheless effective strategies such as this often bring about feelings of fear in the nurse. Fear is an unpleasant, uncomfortable and lonely experience which most people would naturally prefer to avoid, and this is nothing to be ashamed of. Most nurses strive to uphold the professional demands of nursing and their commitment to humanity, but concern for one's own safety is a human need that must be satisfied. Nurses act to support the rights and interests of patients and clients. However, there are some situations in very hostile and dangerous environments where this would almost be an impossibility, and what is important then is that nurses' fears do not prevent them from referring their patient or client to an independent advocacy scheme. Alternatively, if nurses choose to act as advocate for their patient or client, they may well feel that they require extra support and understanding from friends and colleagues. Again nurses must not be afraid to seek independent counselling to support them through such a period. Discussing fears with someone else often puts events into perspective and provides courage for the nurse to proceed.

Helplessness

One of the most destructive and distressing of all emotional responses to acting as advocate is the overwhelming feeling of helplessness, which is well documented within psychological texts. The concept of helplessness is used to describe people who face such overwhelming odds that they feel unable to respond, react, question or challenge the situation in which they find themselves. Atkinson et al (1990) identify studies that demonstrate how people and animals learn to he helpless when faced with stressful situations.

Activity 3.2

The reader is asked to reflect momentarily upon his or her own practice. Try and identify a time when you felt so helpless and unable to challenge the system that you in a sense submitted; you shut down to the possibility of changing things. Discuss the situation with a colleague

and describe how you resolved the situation. If you
have not had such an experience, find a colleague who
has and is prepared to discuss with you the feelings he
or she experienced.

In some environments it is difficult to speak up and represent a patient's rights and interests. The types of environments referred to in chapter 2 (Supportive, Closed and
Hostile or Dangerous) provide both the necessary and sufficient elements to analyse the likely difficulties that may
lead to the feeling of helplessness. Outcomes were also
described that could help prevent the experience of helplessness, by enabling the nurse to identify hostile and
dangerous environments. Instead of nurses simply assum-
ing that it was appropriate for them to act as advocates in
all situations, these outcomes proposed suggestions as to
the safest response they could make to the difficulties
encountered.

Activity 3.3

Spend some time now reflecting on hostile
environments. If you have experience of such
environments or contexts, discuss these with colleagues,
especially those colleagues who have not practised in the
same settings as yourself. Learning from one another's
practice and experience is valuable. It is important that
we do not perpetuate the myth that such environments
do not exist and that such places have nothing to do with
the profession of nursing.

Hostile and dangerous environments do still exist and
nurse practitioners must recognise this and attempt to
guard themselves against becoming helpless practitioners.
Referral by a nurse, if that is what the patient or their
relatives wish, to an independent advocacy scheme or to
another independent practitioner willing to act as advocate
is a positive action. Such an action helps challenge danger-

ous and hostile environments whilst at the same time representing a patient's rights and interests.

Betrayal

Should nurses choose to act as advocates for their patients against the advice or wishes of colleagues and/or the organisation for which they work, they may well experience some form of overt or covert reaction from peers. Examples of these reactions have already been catalogued. Colleagues who pledged their support and help may well retreat to safeguard and protect themselves. Sometimes, when nurses act as advocates they find themselves reflecting on colleagues and friends, who, only a few weeks before the difficult situation, offered comradeship and support. Such comradeship and support often evaporate in the face of adversity. It is at this point that a nurse may well experience an overwhelming feeling of betrayal. To read some, albeit superficial, accounts of nursing and advocacy, one wonders whether some authors have actually spoken out for vulnerable people in difficult circumstances. Carpenter (1992), for example, states that 'Most of the advocacy that a nurse undertakes as part of her professional role involves no conflict at all'.

This statement is disputed. Indeed it is the author's own experience of such conflict that prompted him to become an independent citizen advocate. Conflict is something that most people actively attempt to avoid, using the skills, where necessary, of assertiveness and compromise as alternatives. If one raises, quite rightly, the level of sophistication of debate concerning the practice of advocacy, then conflict is often inevitable. There is a substantial difference between, on the one hand, defending a person's right not to be prescribed powerful neuroleptic medicines or pointing out to a woman that there is an alternative to a radical mastectomy, and, on the other, supporting the desire and possible right of a mother to be visited by her children whilst she is in hospital. In a sense all three examples are equally important but, relatively speaking, the two former examples are extremely complex, involving many disciplines and colleagues. The issues of whether the nurse should support her medical colleague who has prescribed chemotherapy or provide possibly conflicting advice concerning mastectomy are fraught with moral and ethical issues for nurse practitioners.

It is the case that nurses are sometimes betrayed not only by colleagues but also by the profession. There exists a powerful containing force within the nursing profession that promotes the status quo and almost prohibits an acknowledgement that to act as advocate is potentially harmful to one's health. This has led many practitioners to believe that they were safe to act as advocates for their patients. In truth, nurses are often betrayed. Again the reader is asked to reflect upon the examples provided in chapter 2. The experience and feelings of betrayal are difficult to resolve. Nonetheless, it is important to do this. Again, prolonged and possibly damaging feelings of betrayal may necessitate a nurse seeking support through counselling.

Happiness or euphoria

One of the most positive and rewarding experiences, when acting as advocate, is the success of the nurse and patient in upholding their rights and/or interests. It does not matter whether the issue the nurse has represented is large or small; of more significance is establishing the principle that the individual's rights and interests are as important, if not more so, as those of the professions and the organisation caring for that individual. To advocate successfully for someone, achieving the wished-for outcome, is, quite rightly, a time for happiness. However, it is important to remember that each person for whom a nurse speaks out is different. Therefore, being successful once is no guarantee of further success. It is, nonetheless, important to let patients see that it is possible to assert the importance, integrity and uniqueness of each patient being cared for by a nurse.

Advocacy: How Should Nurses Learn?

This final section outlines a proposal for a new and different way for nurses to learn about advocacy. The author has found no research into the ways in which advocacy is taught to nurses, during either pre-registration or post-registration levels of study. Given that there are some 51 260 (DoH 1990) students of nursing taught each year who will be expected to form a part of the nursing work force of 404 000 whole-time equivalent nursing and midwifery staff (DoH 1989), it is imperative that, as a profession, nursing thinks carefully about how advocacy is taught both to the novices and to existing practitioners. The author would suggest that in some ways nurses are ideal people to adopt and practise advocacy, but not necessarily as an integral component of their role. A recent study by O'Brien et al (1992) provides some interesting insights into the characteristics of 'good' advocates. This study sought to identify those personality characteristics of advocates which correlate with the ability to maintain advocacy relationships. The study was conducted in Australia on 59 advocates, of whom 45 were women and 14 were male, with a mean age of 30. An analysis of the occupations of 20 of the advocates is interesting: 4 were from the teaching profession, 4 were from the helping professions and 7 were full-time students. Therefore, 75 per cent of the 20 advocates analysed originated from a professional scenario not too dissimilar from nursing. All

59 advocates had their personality characteristics measured by the California Personality Inventory (CPI). Scores were then used to investigate whether personality characteristics could be used to predict the maintenance of a relationship between the advocate and the protégé. The study found that where relationships lasted beyond eighteen months there was a high degree of flexibility and adaptability in the thinking and social behaviour of the advocate. In addition, advocates demonstrated a sense of wellbeing, freedom from self-doubt and disillusionment, also appearing versatile, productive and energetic. There was also evidence in these advocates of dependability, conscientiousness and common sense. Generally those advocates who were able to maintain long-term partnerships displayed characteristics of flexibility, confidence and common sense. Compare these characteristics to the proposed preparation of Project 2000 students of nursing:

> This means producing flexible practitioners who have the confidence and readiness for change. (UKCC 1986)

It would seem that this new preparation of nurses, whose very education is designed to promote the most positive characteristics for successful advocate partnerships, could make a significant contribution to the field of advocacy. There is much in the substance of nursing and the work of nurses that, potentially, would make them excellent advocates. This observation is offered with the caveat of the author's earlier discussion concerning the potential problems of nurses acting as advocates whilst simultaneously practising nursing. There are three areas of relevance to a discussion on the teaching and learning of advocacy:

- Inappropriateness of the literature;
- Inappropriateness of curriculum design;
- Inappropriateness of the experience of nurse teachers.

Each of these is discussed separately.

Inappropriateness of literature

Because of the absence of relevant research on teaching and learning about advocacy, it is important that these are firmly grounded in good examples of the practice of advocacy, that is, without relevant research it would seem not unreasonable to allow 'good practice' and current theoretical thinking to guide that which is taught. It is clear from the literature that there exists an abundance of problems from the perspectives of patient, nurse, organisation and profession as to the role of the nurse as advocate. For a nurse to act as advocate will prove problematic and this is not always demonstrated in the literature. Concerning nursing, advocacy and children, Barlow (1992) has said:

> The child will frequently require someone to represent his views to other members of the health care team and to act on his behalf. The most appropriate person to undertake this will normally be one of the parents. However, there will be times when advocacy will have to be undertaken by the nurse.

In relation to how the nurse would act as advocate she said:

> The nurse will ensure that the child's progress is reported to other members of the team to ensure that the most appropriate care and treatments are given.
>
> (Barlow 1992)

Bower (1979) has said:

> More recently nurses have assumed the role of consumer advocate.

This unproblematic portrayal of both the adoption and practice of advocacy by nurses is questioned. The literature portrayed in chapter 2 demonstrates the inherent tensions that a nurse may experience, should she choose to act as patient advocate.

Inappropriateness of curriculum design

Nurse educators need to think carefully about how advocacy is taught. This places a responsibility on curriculum planners to ensure that advocacy is taught in relevant and meaningful ways. This is because there exists a gap between the theory and the practice of nursing. This point is not new and yet this gap is perpetuated by heady abstractions in the planning stage of curricula for nursing courses. This point is worth pursuing by way of an example. Benner and Wrubel (1989) provide a clear direction to both an understanding and the practice of nursing through the caring perspective. This caring perspective has of late featured in many nursing curricula, but it is not uncommon to find that this is negated by, for example, other components in the curriculum reinforcing the centrality of professional dimensions to nurses' roles. This, coupled with the theory and practice divide, conspires to form the antithesis of caring. Such internal inconsistency is common in nursing curricula.

Inappropriateness of teacher experience

It is not uncommon to find that nurse teachers, regardless of speciality, have lost touch with some, if not all, aspects of the practice of the profession in which they teach. Given the sometimes tenuous link between a nurse teacher's advice, comments or even knowledge, and an absence of relevant, appropriate or recent experience in nursing, one could level the criticism that they may not always be the most appropriate people to teach or even to facilitate learning concerned with advocacy. Clearly, how successfully a student of nursing can become enthused with the contemporary knowledge and skills of advocacy is in part dependent upon the teacher's own enthusiasm. It is important for nurse teachers to recognise a need to use independent expertise. Whilst nurse teachers are significant and important contributors to the learning process in students of nursing they should not deny students the wider understanding of the theory and practice of advocacy.

The inappropriateness of the literature, curriculum design and teaching of advocacy by nurse teachers having been identified, it would appear necessary to suggest an alternative to the status quo. Just as practitioners may need to seek the advice or services of an independent advocate for their patient or client, so too should those charged with teaching students. Facilitation and/or teaching by service delivery practitioners should be external and independent of the context in which students of nursing learn or work. This could easily be organised through independent advocates or advocacy agencies. Nursing studies departments at Universities and Colleges of Nursing and Midwifery must learn to use known and independent expertise, rather than attempting to teach a broad-based curriculum. It is important that this expertise should be credible and should be able to demonstrate the application of advocacy to professional role issues. Practitioners offering such expertise should be able to demonstrate the ability to network other independent advocacy schemes and personnel. Such a relatively independent educational practice is in keeping with current ideological thought related to patients' rights and *The Patient's Charter* (DoH 1991).

This approach to the teaching of advocacy would achieve two things.

Firstly, it would reinforce and therefore emphasise that for nurses to operate successfully as nurse practitioners in the nineties and beyond, then they must do just that – operate as practitioners. It is important for nurses to develop independence, self-confidence and autonomy, yet, at the same time, demonstrate co-operative practitioner skills. These skills will enable nurses to provide advocacy support and/or the skills to network such support from other practitioner colleagues.

Secondly, the teaching and therefore the promotion of advocacy taught through independent practitioners is an outward sign of commitment, by both the purchaser and provider alike, to providing quality care. It has the potential of being jargon free and requiring no launch of glossy brochures. Those involved in the teaching would provide this advice to customers at a realistic and competitive price. Should the service not meet the specification of the purchaser, then they would simply look to another source for a quality educational programme on advocacy. The content of such an educational programme would inevitably vary across the country and would to a greater extent depend upon the specifications of the purchaser. However, any purchaser of such a programme would need to ensure that thorny and complex areas were included as an integral component of the learning exercise. As far as the purchaser is concerned, it must also be said that an attempt to rely purely on market forces will probably bring criticism concerning the integrity of the educational programme sought. Simply stated, there is more at stake here than profit; sometimes it is morally right to pursue a 'non-accountant' mode of thinking and operation. The proposed educational programme in advocacy would need to address the major dimensions regarding the theory and the practice of advocacy detailed in table 3.1.

Activity 3.4

The reader is invited to reflect upon the identified dimensions of the educational programme comparing and contrasting them with their own experience of learning about advocacy and nursing.

Table 3.1. Proposed dimensions and indicative contents
for the teaching of advocacy

Dimension 1. The concepts and practice of advocacy and
reaffirmation of universal rights for all people.
The nature of universal rights
Legislative differences in rights
Instrumental competency and expressive need
The nature of partnerships

Dimension 2. The various types of advocacy.
Self-advocacy
Citizen advocacy
Legal advocacy
Collective/class advocacy

Dimension 3. An analysis of a professional operating as advo-
cate within a variety of contexts and of the inherent problems.
Role stress and strain
Multiple loyalties and conflict
Dangerous and hostile environments

Dimension 4. The use of networking agencies and other inde-
pendent advocates.
Effective inter-agency communication skills
Assertiveness skills
Negotiating skills

Dimension 5. Dealing with conflict and seeking support during
stressful periods.
Recognition of conflict
Interventions to reduce conflict
Ability to maintain own health

Dimension 6. Evaluation of advocacy schemes.
The nature of evaluation
Quantitative and qualitative approaches
Summative and formative strategies

Conclusion

This chapter commenced with discussion on the role complexities concerning a nurse attempting to act as advocate
whilst simultaneously practising nursing. This led to the
consideration of role conflict and role strain, and to the
proposal that role strain is a predictable outcome of
the different demands that organisational bodies and individuals place upon a practising nurse. It has been acknowledged that nurses may experience a range of consequential
emotional responses, should they choose to act as advocate
for their patient or client. Paradoxically, it has also been
identified that it is possible to experience this same range
of emotional responses, even if nurses choose not to act
as advocate. The author has attempted to avoid giving
specific advice on how to deal with such experiences, as
this is a very specialised area that may require counselling
and support.

However, four important principles are identified that a
nurse should consider before adopting the role of advocate:

1. Accept that it may not always be appropriate for the
    nurse to act as advocate.
2. Recognise that should nurses act as advocates they are
    likely to experience, with some intensity, a range of
    emotional responses to complex and difficult
    situations.
3. Be prepared to discuss feelings experienced with
    trusted colleagues, or seek professional counselling for
    support.
4. Recognise that there is no need to be fearful about or
    ashamed of not defending a patient's rights in person.
    The nurse must learn, instead, to refer the patient to
    an independent advocate or advocacy scheme, should
    difficulties be experienced.

Lastly, proposals for a new and different way both to
teach and to learn about advocacy have been outlined. This

is dependent upon students and practitioners of nursing demanding new, more realistic and meaningful ways to learn about advocacy. Without a belief in patients being able to empower themselves, either through information from nurses or by using nurses to act as their advocates, many current statements purporting to promote patient care and advocacy will be perceived as illusory and empty rhetoric. Chapter 4 considers the ethical dimensions of advocacy and nursing before outlining a new approach to how nurses may practise advocacy whilst excluding some of the difficulties discussed thus far.

References

Abel-Smith B (1987) *A History of the Nursing Profession*. London: Heinemann.

Allmark P and Klarzynski R (1992) The case against nurse advocacy. *British Journal of Nursing*, **2** (1): 33–6.

Atkinson R L, Atkinson R C, Smith E E, Bem D J and Hilgard E R (1990) *Introduction to Psychology* (10th edn). Orlando, Florida: Harcourt Brace Jovanovich.

Barlow S (1992) Children. In Kenworthy N, Snowley G and Gilling C (eds) *Common Foundation Studies in Nursing*. Edinburgh: Churchill Livingstone.

Becker H (1963) *Boys in White*. Chicago: University of Chicago Press.

Benner P and Wrubel J (1989) *The Primacy of Caring: Stress and coping in health and illness*. Menlo Park, California: Addison-Wesley.

Bower F L (1979) Nursing process roles and functions of the nurse. In Bower F L and Bevis E O *Fundamentals of Nursing Practice Concepts, Roles, and Functions*. St Louis: C V Mosby.

Carpenter D (1992) Advocacy. *Nursing Times*, **88** (27): i–viii.

Castledine G (1981) The nurse as the patient's advocate: Pros and Cons. *Nursing Mirror*, **15** (20): 38–40

Clay T (1987) *Nurses, Power and Politics*. London: Heinemann.

Conway M E (1988) Theoretical approaches to the study of roles. In Conway M E and Hardy M E *Role Theory: Perspectives for health professionals* (2nd edn). Norwalk, Connecticut: Appleton-Century-Crofts.

Copp L A (1986) The nurse as advocate for vulnerable persons. *Journal of Advanced Nursing*, **11** (3): 255–63.

DoH (1989) *Working for Patients*. London: HMSO.

DoH (1990) *National Health Service Workforce in England*. London: Department of Health.

DoH (1991) *The Patient's Charter*. London: HMSO.

Durkheim E (1964) *The Division of Labor*. New York: Free Press.

Elkin F and Handel G (1972) *The Child and Society: The process of socialisation* (2nd edn). New York: Random House.

Hardy W L (1988) Role stress and role strain. In Conway M E and Hardy M E *Role Theory: Perspectives for health professionals* (2nd edn). Norwalk, Connecticut: Appleton-Century-Crofts.

Henderson V (1966) *The Nature of Nursing*. New York: Macmillan.

HMSO (1992) The report of the committee of inquiry into allegations of abuse at Ashworth Hospital. London: HMSO.

Lloyd A (1992) The women who dared to speak up. The *Guardian*. 12th August.

Mackay L (1993) *Conflicts in Care. Medicine and nursing*. London: Chapman & Hall.

Meleis A I (1988) *Theoretical Nursing: Development and progress* (2nd edn). New York: J B Lippincott Company.

Melia K (1987) *Learning and Working: The occupational socialisation of nurses*. London: Tavistock.

O'Brien P, Tuck B, Elkins J and Cummins R (1992) Personality characteristics of advocates and maintenance of relationships in a citizen advocacy programme. *The British Journal of Mental Subnormality*, **XXXVIII** (74): 24.

Parsons T (1951) *The Social System*. New York: Free Press.

Spencer M (1979) *Foundations of Modern Sociology* (2nd edn). New Jersey: Prentice Hall.

UKCC (1986) *Project 2000: A new preparation for practice*. London: UKCC.

Webster Universal Dictionary (1975) New York: Harver Educational Services.

CHAPTER 4

The Nurse Advocate and the Caring Ethic

We have now spent some time looking at the issues that surround nurse practitioners who may attempt to enact the role of advocate, and the inherent problems they may face. Besides this discussion, the collective practice of nurses as advocates can also be further contextualised by an understanding of the ethical issues and dilemmas that surround advocacy and nursing.

Ethics, Caring and Advocacy

Before looking at the issues that are central to a discussion on advocacy and nursing it is appropriate to explore briefly the underlying theoretical orientations concerning ethics, as well as the nature of the caring ethic and some of the difficulties that nurses will encounter if this ideology should govern their practice.

Marr (1992) provides a useful summary of two classical theoretical perspectives on ethics. The first of these is known at **utilitarianism** (or **consequentialism**) and is concerned with acts that enable the greatest good for the greatest number. This approach suggests that, where an act produces no good, then at least it should do no harm. There are three general types of utilitarianism:

- Act utilitarianism.
- General utilitarianism.
- Rule utilitarianism

Act utilitarianism.

This relates to assessing a given dilemma and attempting to arrive at some form of optimum balance whereby good would triumph over evil.

General utilitarianism

This is concerned with operationalising utilitarianism, with exploring, hypothetically, the consequences of an action to a particular dilemma.

Rule utilitarianism

This asserts a need to conform to rules that have been established to procure the greatest good for the greatest number.

The second theoretical approach outlined here is that of **deontology** (generically known as **non-consequentialism**). This asserts the duty to arrive at actions that are good, regardless of the consequences. There are two types of deontology:

- Rule deontology.
- Act deontology.

Rule deontology

This states that a given dilemma must be resolved through and within clearly defined rules. There should be no inclusion of extraneous factors when attempting to understand the dilemma. This also means that there should be no idiosyncratic or individualistic interpretation of the pre-defined rules.

Act deontology

Within act deontology there is a promotion of the existential dimension to ethics, that is, each dilemma must be judged and resolved within the temporal dimension of the 'here and now'.

It is useful to compare and contrast these two different theoretical perspectives. In utilitarianism the underlying ideology is concerned with the greatest good for the greatest number, with acknowledgement and understanding of the consequences of actions and the need to conform to rules. In deontology there is an emphasis upon the resolution of dilemmas in the present, a pursuit of good for its own sake regardless of the consequences. It is only in rule deontology that there appears to be a similarity between the two approaches. This similarity is concerned with following rules, although it must be said that in deontology goodness is still pursued in preference to concerns of consequence.

As with all theoretical approaches they provide nurses with a framework of reference; however, such approaches cannot be equally applicable in all the multiplicity of contexts in which nurse practitioners may work. Nurses need to be able to analyse and synthesise the theoretical approaches and then to assimilate and accommodate the outcome of this process into reflective practice. Tschudin (1992) has acknowledged the difficulties of following a single theoretical approach: 'It seems difficult to act without thinking of the consequences at all, or to act thinking only of the consequence'.

Such a point of view was supported by Ellis (1993) who argued for a combined view of the theoretical perspectives: 'The most satisfactory way of resolving ethical dilemmas is to combine the best features of both utility and deontology. Applying this sort of combined view of ethics enables professionals to act within the confines of their code of conduct and take account of their own beliefs and cultural/sociological influences as well as those of their clients'.

The relationship between caring and ethics in nursing has been explored by Tschudin (1986). The nature of caring is portrayed as the nurse being in a relationship with another human being. In the caring relationship there is respect for the other person and clarity of the relationship between nurse and patient. In addition, the caring relationship enables the other person to express him/herself freely. It also enables the nurse to empathise with the patient, but it is suggested there is a need for the nurse to retain a separateness so as not to be overwhelmed. Lastly, the relationship should enable the other person to grow and develop as a human being, with the nurse communicating support for this person. In a sense, the promotion of caring in nursing is a renaissance of the fundamental nature of nursing. It is to do with a deep and profound concern for humanity that transcends contracts and the current ideology of the 'market place' within health care. Brown, Kitson and McKnight (1992) have suggested that caring will manifest itself at a natural and ethical level. Concerning the natural level they said: 'If we did not want to care and be cared for, if we did not mind suffering and were not liable to despair or if such experiences could not be helped by companionship, then we would not need to put such a high value on caring'. This natural level of caring enables the nurse to develop an ethic of caring. At the ethical level of caring they suggested that 'the basic notions of caring supply a form that impulses can take which would otherwise be formless and to facilitate good before one's own is a clear declaration of one's ethical position' (Brown, Kitson and McKnight 1992).

Curtin (1979) argued that advocacy was a philosophical foundation and ideal of nursing within the caring ethic:

'Perhaps the philosophical foundation and ideal of nursing is the nurse as advocate. This concept is not simply one more alternative to be added to the list of past and present concepts of nursing nor does it reject any of them – it embraces all of them' (Curtin 1979). In developing her argument of this idea of the nurse as advocate she said: 'This proposed ideal of advocacy is based upon our common humanity, our common needs and our common rights. We are human beings, our patients or clients are human beings, and it is this commonalty that should form the basis of the relationship between us. It often seems that we have permitted traditionalism, elitism and more recently legalism to obscure this most basic of facts' (Curtin 1979).

Clearly such a position was grounded in the caring ethic. A commitment to the caring ethic would appear to value and promote a more subjective mode of caring in nursing as opposed to the more objective and distancing mode of nursing. Such commitment to caring will require the nurse to give of herself in the truest sense. This giving will inevitably extend beyond the fixed requirements of professional codes and contracts and, because of this, there may be a personal cost to the nurse practitioner.

An opposing argument to the caring ethic questions the authenticity of caring. This argument raises as problematic whether the nature of caring has been professionalised or in a sense institutionalised by the nursing profession. Is caring in this case no more than a convenient display of concern, with little or no depth to the relationship, as compared to the love between a mother and her child or a husband and his wife? There may be a substantive difference between the professional nature of caring as enacted by a nurse, and the caring that is found in true, deeply personal social relationships. Brown, Kitson and McKnight (1992) discussed this issue at length making a distinction between the lay and professional values in a caring relationship. Melia (1987) pointed out a number of differences between caring and nursing. Firstly, nursing is a paid and contracted service between an employer and an employee (the nurse). Secondly, nurses are not involved in the other person's life on an individual basis, as are family and friends. Lastly, Melia suggested that there is often an incongruity between the nurse's values, life style and culture and those of the person she is nursing. Given these potential differences and difficulties, one might legitimately ask whether it is possible for a nurse to adopt the caring ethic as it is portrayed in the literature.

Activity 4.1

The reader is asked to spend some time reflecting on the two ethical perspectives and the nature of caring so far outlined. The following tasks should then be attempted:
1. Briefly describe deontology.
2. Briefly describe utilitarianism.
3. Briefly describe caring.

Having briefly explored two theoretical perspectives concerning ethics and the nature of caring, let us now consider a model of deliberation that nurses might use in resolving ethical dilemmas as to whether or not they could or should act as patient advocate, and whether their decisions could be ethically justified.

Brown, Kitson and McKnight (1992) outlined a series of stages that a nurse should follow when faced with ethical dilemmas:

1. Appreciation of the situation and possible outcomes.
2. Review of possible courses of action.
3. Selection and application of principles.
4. Weighing of practical considerations.
5. Decision.

Stage 1

This stage requires a practitioner to identify and prioritise the elements of a situation that presents itself as a dilemma. The process of prioritising requires identification of the important features of the dilemma and those that could be thought of as marginal.

Stage 2

The nurse practitioner is required to map out the various courses of action that could be pursued.

Stage 3

In this stage the nurse practitioner must consider the dilemma in the light of his/her own principles, which originate, for example, from experience, the caring ethic and the professional code of conduct. These principles will lead the practitioner to consider a particular course of action.

Stage 4

Here practitioners are required to consider their proposed response within the context in which they are currently working, and the consequences that may be experienced if they pursue that response.

Stage 5

The final stage is essentially the decision-making stage. It was proposed that the practitioner of nursing would make an informed decision on the basis of a clearly defined process of deliberation as opposed to a reflex reaction.

This process of deliberation has been presented in a greatly simplified and linear manner. In true deliberation, resolution of dilemmas is probably more spiral in nature than linear. Thus the process is more sophisticated and dynamic than portrayed here, with the various stages being revisited on more than one occasion before a decision is reached.

Activity 4.2

From the description provided of this model of deliberation, the reader is asked to identify the theoretical perspective of ethics to which it applies.

In deciding whether or not to act as a patient advocate, the nurse faces an unenviable ethical dilemma. There are no easy answers to such dilemmas, which is why the use of a structured process of deliberation is advised.

Clearly to sustain a caring relationship will require a deep commitment from the nurse. However, the author would argue that when the caring relationship is put into a context, such as the nurse acting as advocate, then problems begin to surface that make the sometimes heady rhetoric of caring very problematic. It is clearly important that nurses act in a manner that promotes their beneficent role, meaning that their actions should be undertaken for the good of the patient. This is opposed to the nurse acting in a maleficent manner, one that may be seen as harmful to the patient. It should be asked, however, is the decision not to act as advocate a maleficent act that demonstrates non-commitment to the caring ethic?

Activity 4.3

The reader is invited to read the following case history and then deliberate whether the nurse should act as advocate.
The reader should reflect on the theoretical models of ethics and the nature of caring, already briefly outlined, and:

1. Identify which of the theoretical perspectives of ethics informed your decision-making process and,
2. Describe how the caring ethic has been upheld through the decision you have reached.

Len was a sixty-four year old man who was admitted to a London teaching hospital from a provincial hospital because of the need for specialist services. Len had a history of cardiovascular problems that culminated, two years before this admission, in his undergoing surgery for a coronary bypass operation. Recently he had been experiencing severe thoracic pain whilst undertaking any physical activity. On admission to the coronary care unit, he was diagnosed as having unstable angina. On the following day he was moved from the unit to another ward without any explanation. Whilst on this ward he was told he would have to have an angiogram. On the next day Len had his angiogram performed. Following this he was seen by a 'woman in a white coat', whom he assumed to be a doctor, and was told that his bypass had become 'diseased and then disintegrated'. He was then told that this would be explained to him on the following day during the doctor's rounds. He spent the next day until 7 p.m., when the doctor eventually saw him, worrying about what was wrong with him. The doctor who saw Len informed him that he would have to have an angioplasty. The following day he was moved from his ward yet again, this time to an ear, nose and throat ward. Len began, at this point, to worry that he was only being moved about because they (the medical and nursing staff) were waiting for him to die. He was eventually moved back to the coronary care unit, where he was taken to theatre for his operation. The following day, after his return from theatre, he and his wife complained to you, his named nurse, that he felt desperately uncared for and confused, and he asked you to do something about it.

Is it possible for the nurse to sustain an authentic caring relationship with a patient whilst acting as advocate and at the same time practise in an ethically appropriate way? Is it not the case that, when professional, contextual and a multitude of other factors conspire against the nurse and patient, this may prevent the development of a caring relationship?

The next section of this chapter outlines a new approach to how a nurse may adopt the role of advocate whilst maintaining a caring relationship.

A New Nurse for a New World

Having discussed the problems of advocacy and the forming of meaningful, caring relationships or partnerships with our patients it is now necessary to consider in some detail a new and different way in which nurses can act as advocates. In short, a vision for a new practitioner of nursing for the nineties and beyond is required. In an important document by the King's Fund Institute, Beardshaw and Robinson (1990) described a new ideology for nursing:

> The new nursing is shorthand for a complex, multifaceted movement to change the basis of current nursing practice . . . it seeks to substitute a professional model of organisation for nursing's long established hierarchical, bureaucratic one. Its proponents base the new approach on a highly skilled nurse practitioner who will have the competence and self-confidence to plan, give, supervise and evaluate care tailored precisely to the needs of individual patients.

Such a visionary ideology is in keeping with the emergence of a true practitioner. Central to the independence of a practitioner is the right to practise a variety of competency-based skills for the growth, independence and holistic healing of patients or clients. In other words, nurses, as potentially independent practitioners, should not be constrained to the current image of nursing. In addition, they should be empowered to use their wealth of skills and knowledge outside the 'work context'. This could be achieved by the establishment of independent collaborative nursing advocacy schemes. This new and different way in which nurses could act as advocates is to be described later in this chapter. Such an innovation would be in the interests not only of patients and clients but also of nurse practitioners. This is because they could practise, safe in the knowledge that their colleagues could support their patient or client by offering truly independent advocacy should they require it. This is especially relevant when organisational or professional problems make it difficult for nurses to act in the capacity of advocate. Beardshaw and Robinson (1990) acknowledged this difficulty and said:

> while it is currently fashionable for health care
> professionals to advocate 'partnership' with patients . . .
> changing the traditional basis of the relationship between
> professional and client often proves difficult in practice.

The slow development and emergence of a practitioner of nursing, during the twentieth century, can be seen as an attempt to move toward patient-centred nursing. The word 'nursing' is used deliberately, but the author reinforces the importance of recognising 'caring' as the single most important component of nursing. However, nurses must be wary not to allow the current-day rhetoric of caring to reduce the significance or importance of nursing. Caring is an activity that can be undertaken by a variety of professions. Indeed Benner and Wrubel (1989) talked of universal human caring skills. Such skills are neither denied, nor is their concept criticised. However, caring within the framework of the nursing profession takes on a new dimension. It is the 'nursing' that makes the care different. Let us briefly study the dimensions of traditional and patient–centred nursing as identified by Beardshaw and Robinson (1990) and shown in table 4.1.

Activity 4.4

You are invited to spend some time reflecting on the contents of table 4.1 and comparing and contrasting some of the statements made with your current practice or experience as a student or practitioner of nursing. You should then attempt the following questions:
1. As a student or practitioner of nursing do you think your practice as a nurse is traditional or have you moved to patient-centred nursing?
2. As a student or practitioner of nursing you should be able to reflect on a number of different specialities and contexts in which you have worked. What are your impressions of the role of the nurse and the role of the patient in those different contexts and specialities? Attempt to discuss your experience with colleagues and peers. Reflect deeply on experience, and ask yourself why it is that in some contexts in which you have worked, nursing is practised in a particular way.

Table 4.1 clearly draws together a number of threads from our discussions thus far. It acknowledges a shift from tired patterns of nursing care provision to new and innovative patterns of care, which would support and enable the emergence of truly independent practitioners of nursing. It is the independent practice of nursing that is central to our ability as nurses to act as advocates for our patients and clients. It has already been established that to act as advocate in some work contexts is made impossible by the combination of conflicts of loyalty and closed, hostile or dangerous environments. This combination of professional demand, role complexity and the environment in which nurses practise, can be demonstrated in the Bermuda Triangle of Nursing (figure 4.1).

Table 4.1 Traditional and patient-centred nursing (after Beardshaw & Robinson 1990).

TRADITIONAL NURSING

PATIENT-CENTRED NURSING

The role of the nurse:
Nurses assume a variety of tasks, generally following ward and hospital routines. They are constantly directed in their activities.
Competence is relative, and just surviving in the work place is the 'order of the day'.

Qualified nurses are empowered and have authority to plan, implement and evaluate care plans based on individual needs of patients or clients.
Therapeutic role is grounded in practitioner competence and based upon independent practice.

Division of labour:
Unqualified staff provide nursing care; qualified nurses supervise.

Qualified nurses plan and implement care supported by a range of unqualified caring staff.

Role of ward sister/charge nurse:
The ward sister/charge nurse establishes ward routine, liaises with medical and other senior health staff and undertakes, with the 'caring team', a variety of administrative, housekeeping and clerical duties.

The charge nurse/ward sister is seen as the consultant practitioner and is able to manage a ward team and to co-ordinate staff development.

Role of the patient:
The patient is seen as a passive recipient of care.

The patient or client is seen as an active partner in planning care to meet individual needs.

Role of nursing management:
Manages nursing establishment, exercising authority over independent practitioners.

Managers act as enablers. Practitioners are encouraged to learn, take risks and provide innovative care.

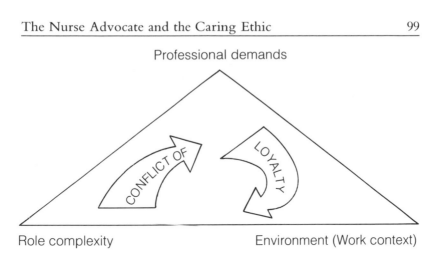

Figure 4.1 The Bermuda Triangle of Nursing.

If nurses were able to break free from the constraints of the triangle, it would be possible to adopt a variety of advocate roles, dependent upon a nurse's expertise – for example, citizen, self, collective and possibly legal advocacy. Failure to break free of the triangle will result in advocacy being lost in the Bermuda Triangle of Nursing.

Before moving this discussion forward, it important to try to understand that what is proposed is a legitimate claim for nurses. If nurses claim their role to be that of promoting 'holistic health and the care of people', then they must face their responsibilities and offer more than the substance of their contracts.

This chapter continues by discussing the where, when, how and why of a new vision of advocacy for practitioners of nursing. Bearing in mind earlier discussions concerning multiple conflicts and loyalties, any new vision for the practice of advocacy by a nurse needs to be conceptualised in such a way as to minimise conflict. There would appear to be two alternatives open to nurse practitioners in achieving this aim.

The first option is joining existing citizen advocacy schemes, offering their nurse practitioner expertise. Such expertise would be offered in partnership with those people who would most benefit from their particular practitioner skills. Therefore, a nurse could practise as an advocate for people in their homes, National Health Service trusts, Social Education Centres or indeed in any setting where there is a need for their unique contribution. As each of the National Health Service trusts or units where a nurse could practise as advocate is relatively independent from their own place of practice, issues related to the difficulty of speaking up for another are significantly reduced. Likewise other practitioners within these contexts, no matter how hostile, cannot really harm the nurse. However, if an incestuous relationship still existed between units, then it would be possible for a nurse to act as advocate within a neighbouring Health Authority. This would reduce the degree of conflict so much that it could reasonably be accepted or tolerated.

The second option, and perhaps the bolder form of advocacy practice for nurses, could be a collaborative arrangement between practitioners from all specialities of nursing. Such a collaborative group could form an independent, voluntary advocacy service. In essence the scheme could model itself upon a citizen advocacy ethos. To establish a collaborative advocacy scheme as a voluntary organisation, it would be necessary for a group of nurses to form an embryo of people and ideas into one of five different types of structure:

1. An unregistered association.
2. A trust.
3. A friendly society.
4. A limited company.
5. An industrial and provident society.

The decision concerning the type of structure of such an advocacy scheme is important. This is especially so if the group will be attempting to secure some form of funding to assist with the running costs of the scheme. Most of the grant-offering institutions will offer money only to registered charities. It is also important to be aware that there exists legislation governing the conduct of voluntary organisations. Having established the type of voluntary organisation that the scheme will be, it is essential that the originators of the scheme establish a steering committee, which must be fully committed to the principles of citizen advocacy, and must have at its disposal the broad range of knowledge, skills, leadership and motivating attributes required for the development of such a scheme. O'Brien and Wolfensberger (1979) in their document on standards for advocacy schemes identified the following guidelines:

> A citizen advocacy programme should share few or no aspects of governance with an organisation providing case management services to actual or potential [partners]. An advocacy office should have a governing board which does not have responsibilities for the provision of direct services to actual or potential [partners].

These points are extremely important. Relatively complete independence from care service agencies is required if the scheme is to operate for the benefit of people.

Following on the establishment of the type of structure the scheme will adopt, it is important to construct a constitution by which it will operate. Such a constitution will require the committee to formulate a number of governing principles. It is important for the steering committee to decide with whom they are principally going to act as partners. Many advocacy schemes attempt to provide partnerships for all people, regardless of the scheme's resources or expertise. This can sometimes result in being 'Jack of all trades but master of none'. Therefore, it is important to include this in the scheme's constitution, which should also refer to the name of the scheme, the geographical area

that it will serve, the objectives, the membership and lastly
the rules and regulations by which the scheme will abide.
The steering committee also needs to agree how they are
going to attract nurse practitioners or students of nursing
to join the scheme as advocates. Lastly, it is necessary for
the scheme to establish some formal written co-operative
agreement between the scheme itself and the service-
providing agencies. Such an agreement must state the
extent of the advocate's role; this affords protection from
over-zealous practitioners whose commitment can sometimes be destructive.

Once an individual seeks the help of an advocacy
scheme, the establishment of a partnership should commence as soon as is practicably possible. In the case of
the collaborative advocacy arrangement between nurses,
a response from the scheme could and should be made
with a sense of urgency. When people approach an advocacy scheme they are often tired and demoralised. Because
of this they need a rapid positive response to help restore
their self-confidence and, in the widest sense, to enable
the commencement of true healing to occur. Clearly,
within such a short text as this, it is only possible to
provide a thumb-nail sketch of the process involved in
establishing the proposed collaborative scheme. There are
numerous guidelines available for the setting up of advocacy schemes, two publishers being:

> The London Voluntary Service Council, 68 Chalton
> Street, London, NW1 1JR. (*Voluntary but not Amateur*)
> The Advocacy Alliance, 16 Chenies Street, London,
> WC1E 7ET.

A proposed way in which nurses could work as independent advocates having been discussed, the remaining part
of this section portrays a recent case history of a partnership from the author's own experience. The example
offered is of a man with whom the author has recently

been working as his independent advocate. This man and his family were introduced to the author through a local advocacy scheme known as CALL (Citizen Advocacy Lincoln Link). This scheme uses the expertise of its advocates as part of the criteria for matching up partnerships. All advocates work voluntarily. The author offers his services as an independent nurse practitioner which include a wide range of skills that extend beyond and transcend the previously discussed skills of traditional or task-allocated nursing. As he did not work within the local Health Authority at the time of this partnership, he experienced no conflict of interest.

The Story of John

John had severe epilepsy which was the direct result of a motor bike accident some twenty years ago. The author was asked to act as a partner and advocate for John to obtain for him a severe disablement allowance. John's social worker had been in the process of attempting to obtain this benefit, when he had to leave the case because of a change in employment. His new social worker felt unable to represent him adequately because of the complexities of his problems. Because of this she sought the help of an independent advocacy scheme. During the first meeting with John a number of important facts were established. Firstly, he had been experiencing some five or six tonic-clonic seizures a day for the last five years. During these seizures he had sustained a horrific catalogue of injuries that included severe bodily lacerations caused by falling through a plate glass door, splitting his nose open, numerous fractures and dislocating his thumb so severely that it had to be wired into place, requiring a period of hospitalisation. Besides this, there was evidence from his wife that John had undergone a significant personality change over the last twenty years, causing him to be irrational and at times lash out at his wife. His wife had decided to commence working nights so that she could attend to John during the day, when he had most of the seizures. Much of the family home had been modified to reduce the risk of injury to John during a seizure. Before John's social worker had left this case he had made contact with the Disablement Resettlement Officer, the British Epilepsy Association and John's own General Practitioner. All of these people had confirmed, in writing, that the nature of John's epilepsy was, in their opinion, severely disabling. The severe disablement allowance was a tax-free benefit for people who had not worked for at least 28 weeks because of illness or disablement. People seeking this allowance would do so because they were unable to claim sickness benefit or invalidity benefit, having made insufficient National Insurance contributions. The great difficulty with this allowance was that if individuals became disabled after their twentieth birthday then they had to be assessed as 80 per cent disabled to obtain the allowance.

John was assessed initially by an independent medical officer as 40 per cent disabled. This meant that he did not qualify for the severe disablement allowance and there was, therefore, an implicit assumption that he was able to work. All who knew John, including the Disablement Resettlement Officer, were quite sure that this assessment was wrong and that his epilepsy was so severe as to prevent him from seeking any form of employment. We (John, his wife and the author) decided that we would appeal against the assessment in the belief that John was 80 per cent disabled. The author spent a series of evenings with John and his wife, getting to know them and their family circumstances. His wife, during all the author's visits to the home, appeared tired and cynical and was, understandably, demoralised and had lost all hope of (as she would frequently say) 'Winning a fair decision. There's them who don't miss out on anything and there is nothing wrong with them!'

We decided that we needed to use all the evidence gathered by their social worker and prepare a case that would leave any medical tribunal in little doubt that John's claim was a fair and reasonable attempt to secure an allowance to which he was entitled. We jointly made notes and we all agreed that the author would present the facts at the medical tribunal. Before the tribunal, the author spent many evenings at home rehearsing arguments, checking facts and mentally preparing himself for the best way in which to present the case. At relatively short notice we were informed of the date of the tribunal, this being the following week from the date of the received letter. It was to be held some fifty miles from John's home. On the day of the tribunal both John and his wife were very tired. John's wife had been working the previous night and John was recovering from an injury to his arm following a seizure. In fact, he had been discharged from the hospital only two days before. The author presented the case to the tribunal, drawing upon his knowledge of and expertise in the management of epilepsy, as well as his skills in effective communication and his ability to read the highly complicated documentation supplied by the Social Security Office. All of these skills and knowledge were directly attributable to his practice of nursing over a number of years. The tribunal appeared to proceed well. However, one of the medical members was concerned about the chemotherapy and its management of the frequency of the seizures John was experiencing. Afterwards we were told that we would have to wait a period of some six to eight weeks before we received a decision. John's wife left the tribunal very dejected. She commented, 'It'll be like all the rest [their attempts to secure some form of benefit]. We end up with nothing and they go home to their posh homes . . . we'll not get anything'.

We received the outcome of the tribunal six weeks later. The medical tribunal ruled against the original assessment and the recommendation from the Secretary of State. The tribunal ruled that John was entitled to a severe disablement allowance and he was assessed as 80 per cent disabled. The ruling got better. The decision was back-dated two years to the period of the first application for the allowance, and lastly the period of disability was calculated until the year 2004, this being the year that John was due to retire.

One should never assume that without one's own personal intervention there would not have been a similar outcome. This said, the author is confident that the partnership that he was able to develop with John and his wife, together with his nursing knowledge and expertise, enabled him to present a coherent well-thought-out case, which the tribunal would have had difficulty in dismissing. The severe disablement allowance has made a significant difference to the quality of the family life and has enabled them to rebuild their self-respect. Hopefully, it has also enabled them to perceive professionals, at least nurses, as people who do care and who are willing to speak up for others.

A True Practitioner

In this penultimate section of this chapter, it is necessary to reaffirm the ideology underlying the proposal for a new form for the practice of advocacy by nurse practitioners. Of necessity, through a complex combination of professional conflict, role strain, employer and employee difficulties, contextual (environmental) difficulties, and conflicts of loyalty, nurses often have to retreat from a true partnership of commitment with their patient. The proposed model of a collaborative advocacy service by nurses is clearly different from the current scenario experienced by nurses and patients. The continued development, both theoretically and practically, of this type of role is important to the continued development of nursing as an independent profession (Audit Commission 1991). There is evidence that some nurses are disaffected with some aspects of their current role. A survey by the Royal College of Nursing (Waite, Buchan and Thomas 1989) revealed some interesting insights into the feelings of qualified nurses in the National Health Service and those working outside the Health Service. Nurses in the Health Service reported that they had 'less experience of doing a worthwhile job, but more inclined to stress and petty regulations' (Waite, Buchan and Thomas 1989).

Mackay (1989) pointed to the repressive influence of nursing hierarchies and identified qualitative components from transcripts of interviews with nurses: 'I'm not frightened of saying what I think . . . but I think if I said too much it wouldn't go down well and some people would close ranks and you get labelled as a trouble maker'.

The author has argued that nurses must push back the frontiers of their role as advocates and by doing this they could significantly affect the quality of life for thousands of people who are leading a disadvantaged or vulnerable existence. The establishment of collaborative nursing advocacy schemes, truly built upon partnerships between patients, clients and practitioners or students of nursing, is an element of total care that is at present absent from much of the practice of nursing. It is imperative for us, from the point of view of this century and the next, to be quite clear as to the role of the nurse in bringing about 'true caring'. True caring transcends contracts, professional obligations and relationships with colleagues. The proposal outlined in this chapter is not some altruistic notion that advocates the emergence of 'do-gooders'. As a profession nursing can reclaim an affirmative belief from the general public that nurses do care, and that they are prepared to stand up and speak out for people in all contexts, concerning any aspect of care that may be detrimental to an individual's holistic maintenance of health. How may nurses practise the art and science of nursing, when the very real issues discussed and portrayed within this book make the practice of advocacy by nurses impossible? Nurses are prevented from being able to act as patient advocates by a conspiracy, of which some elements are contrived and others are natural circumstances. Mahler (1983), in relation to the required changes in the role of the nurse, said:

> The role of the nurse will change, more will move away
> from the hospitals to the everyday life where they are badly
> needed. They will become resources to people rather than
> resources to physicians, becoming more active in educating
> people on health matters . . . if the millions of nurses in
> a thousand places articulate the same ideas and come
> together as a force, then they could act as a power house
> for change. I believe such a change is coming.

This statement projected a positive image of the potential for nursing, an image where professional internal squabbling will become unnecessary baggage of the past. Nursing will move forward in new and exciting ways, which will transcend role boundaries and will have more to do with 'caring for people', the true vocation of nursing, as opposed to nurses being manipulated into roles as agents of governments. Clay (1987) noted that what the nursing profession wanted for nursing had to be congruent with the health needs of society. To maintain or actualise holistic health for society, it is sometimes necessary for practitioners of nursing to stand up and advocate for people in pursuance of their rights and interests. This chapter has attempted to demonstrate how this may be achieved by the realistic development of collaborative nursing advocacy schemes. Such schemes will minimise the professional conflicts so often referred to in this book, thereby maximising the effects of the fundamental basis of nursing, which is simply to care for people.

Conclusion

This chapter has demonstrated, following a brief outline of ethics and caring, how a nurse can practise and advocate for her patient. The approach outlined attempts to resolve the tensions that exist between the ethic of caring and the everyday experience and contexts in which nurses must make decisions. The practice of nursing should be based upon autonomy, co-operativeness, competence and confidence. Above all else the nurse must be able to demonstrate true caring skills that transcend existing role boundaries, contexts of employment, professional de-mands and conflicts of loyalty. In other words, nurses must break free from the Bermuda Triangle of Nursing (figure 4.1). To this end the proposed model for the estab-lishment of collaborative nursing advocacy schemes be-tween nurses will facilitate the advancement and fulfilment of patients' rights and interests. Such a scheme should be based upon a voluntary model, in which nurses would provide such services in the knowledge that they would be able to make reciprocal use of such a scheme to rep-resent their own patients or clients, when a range of diffi-culties may prevent the nurses from acting as advocates themselves. It has also been suggested that, without a move to a truly patient-centred approach to nursing, nurses will continue to be thwarted from practising in a truly independent manner.

The last chapter of this book will explore how nurses

may evaluate the existence, adequacy and promotion of advocacy for their patients and clients. The existence of advocacy provision is not sufficient; there must also be some formal mechanism for evaluating such schemes. Such evaluation is important at the levels of the individual practitioners, the advocacy schemes and the proposed collaborative nursing advocacy schemes. If nurses act as advocates they should be able to evaluate their own deficits and strengths in their provision of advocacy. Similarly, before making any referral to an independent advocacy scheme, nurses must ensure that the scheme has advocates who are both competent and sufficiently resourced to offer a meaningful partnership of help. Lastly, if nurses are to establish new and independent collaborative nursing advocacy schemes, then they must be able to evaluate the effectiveness and efficiency of the scheme in meeting the needs of partnerships. Nurses clearly have skills in the area of evaluating care; these skills are transferable to the context of evaluating advocacy provision and practice.

References

Audit Commission (1991) *The Virtue of Patients: Making best use of ward nursing resources*. London: HMSO.

Beardshaw V and Robinson R (1990) *New for Old? Prospects for nursing in the 1990s*. London: King's Fund Institute.

Benner P and Wrubel J (1989) *The Primacy of Caring: Stress and coping in health and illness*. Menlo Park, California: Addison--Wesley.

Brown J, Kitson A and McKnight T (1992) *Challenges in Caring: Explorations in nursing and ethics*. London: Chapman and Hall.

Clay T (1987) *Nurses, Power and Politics*. London: Heinemann.

Curtin L (1979) The nurse as advocate: A philosophical foundation for nursing. *Advances in Nursing Science*, **1** (3): 1–10

Ellis P (1993) Role of ethics in modern health care: 1. *British Journal of Nursing*, **2** (2): 144–6.

Mackay L (1989) *Nursing a Problem*. Milton Keynes: Open University Press.

Mahler H (1983) Nurses lead the way. In DHSS *A strategy for nursing*. London: DHSS.

Marr J (1992) Morals and ethics in nursing. In Kenworthy N, Snowley G and Gilling C (eds) *Common Foundation Studies in Nursing*. Edinburgh: Churchill Livingstone.

Melia K (1987) *Learning and Working: The occupational socialisation of nurses*. London: Tavistock.

O'Brien J and Wolfensberger W (1979) *Standards for Citizen Advocacy Programme Evaluation (CAPE)*. Toronto: Canadian Association for the Mentally Retarded.

Tschudin V (1986) *Ethics in Nursing: The caring relationship*. London: Heinemann.

Tschudin V (1992) *Ethics in Nursing: The caring relationship* (2nd edn). Oxford: Butterworth Heinemann.

Waite, R, Buchan J and Thomas J (1989) *Nurses in and out of work*. A tracing study 1986–1988 for the Royal College of Nursing of the attitudes, employment and mobility rates of RCN members. IMS report No 170. Institute of Manpower Studies, Brighton University, Sussex.

CHAPTER 5

Evaluating Advocacy and Advocacy Schemes: A Blueprint for Excellence in Care

This final chapter explores a range of approaches that a nurse may use to evaluate the provision and adequacy of advocacy services. These approaches involve two different levels of definition – the first concerned with the individual nurse practitioner, and the second with the organisation. The organisational level of definition will be applied to the new and collaborative scheme of nurse advocacy that has already been outlined in chapter 4. Conceptualising these two levels of definition is rather like looking through a microscope at a prepared slide of blood cells – the higher the level of magnification, the higher the level of definition, resulting in increased insights. This approach to portraying different levels of definition is adopted by Walton (1986), who uses the terms **micro** and **macro level**. At the micro level, a nurse learns from her evaluation of patient care how it may be improved for the next patient. At the macro level, there is consideration of issues such as the organisation of nursing management, the context of care, support services and a myriad of other variables that contribute to the quality of nursing care. This concern with the quality of care has been seen by some as a legitimate role of the advocate (Abrams 1978 and

McKinley 1986). There is a strong emphasis in this chapter on the individual level of definition; this will help the reader to evaluate in some depth both his or her contribution to the promotion of advocacy and the existing skill base of enacting the role of advocate.

The Nature of Evaluation

The Audit Commission (1991) has described evaluation as:

> Appraisal, against a set of criteria, of the effectiveness of the nursing care delivered to a patient in achieving specified goals. The evaluation may show that his care plan needs to be changed or updated.

This is a useful definition with which to commence a discussion on evaluation. However, it fails to address a division in theoretical assumptions concerning its nature. Luker (1981) states that:

> Evaluation is used widely and confusingly in the literature from the everyday sense of making judgements of worth to that of a research concept implying the use of scientific methods and measurements.

Evaluation may be said to be a quantitative and/or qualitative exercise undertaken to measure the relative strengths or limitations of a particular nursing strategy. Evaluation attempts to ask value questions concerning, for example, the effectiveness, efficiency, or economic benefits of a particular strategy or strategies. Such an exercise may be undertaken by attempting to measure the relative success of a strategy against predetermined goals or objectives. This may be referred to as an empirical approach. An example of this may be that of a nurse practitioner attempting to measure the strengths and weaknesses of nursing care provided for a patient. The outcomes of the patient's episode of nursing care could be measured and compared with the defined goals of the care plan. This approach to evaluation is essentially concerned with outcomes.

Alternatively, nurses could describe in more qualitative terms the experience of their patient or client, the nursing interventions and the perceived strengths and weaknesses of the nursing care. This is referred to as an illuminative approach and is essentially concerned with the processes of care.

Regardless of whether a quantitative or qualitative approach is used, it is important to consider the timing of evaluation. Should evaluation be undertaken at the end of an episode of nursing care, or is it a process that should be undertaken continuously? Within this consideration of evaluation it is necessary to discuss the concept of **formative** and **summative evaluation**. Formative evaluation concerns activities that are undertaken on a continuous basis throughout the process of care. This is what Walton (1986) refers to as 'collecting information which can be used mainly for ongoing programme development and improvement'. Summative evaluation, by way of contrast, relates to a process that is undertaken at the end of an episode of care. Walton (1986) refers to this as 'evaluation aimed primarily at making an overall judgement about the effectiveness of a programme'.

Given this temporal dimension to the process of evaluation, it would appear that a nurse could undertake evaluation on an almost continuous basis that would include a final overall judgement on the quality of nursing care provided for a patient. Both approaches, regardless of this temporal dimension, appear to be governed by the theoretical assumptions and beliefs underpinning each of the perspectives. Broadly speaking, these perspectives may be placed under the headings of quantitative and qualitative evaluation. These two types of evaluation are now described in more detail.

Quantitative Approach

Central to this approach of evaluation is measurement of outcomes against the predetermined goals of a particular nursing strategy. This approach requires that goals are stated in an unambiguous way so that carefully measured indices can be used to evaluate both the success, or otherwise, and the value, of that strategy. O'Brien (1987) states that 'without observable and measurable objectives, evaluation is at best extremely difficult and at worst impossible and meaningless'.

Miller (1984) showed that the use of the nursing process as compared with task allocation (discussed in chapter 4) did not significantly affect the short-term nursing care of elderly patients. Hawthorn (1984) identified that, following the introduction of the nursing process, fifteen minutes of extra nursing care were given by nurses to patients, and there was a higher nurse-patient ratio. Binnie (1982) noted that, after implementation of the nursing process, more attention was given to individuals' needs, coupled with better communication between nursing staff and improved job satisfaction. Whitfield (1985) recorded that, after the introduction of the nursing process, less routinised care and a greater involvement of relatives in providing nursing care were found. Each of these cited examples illustrates a commitment to the measurement of the outcomes of nursing care in a quantitative manner. They attempt to evidence, by using an empirical approach, that clearly defined objectives for nursing care can be evaluated by studying the outcomes of a particular nursing strategy.

Qualitative Approach

Central to this approach of evaluation is an attempt to illuminate the process of a particular strategy. Emphasis is placed upon understanding, interpretation and the seeking of meaning to the process of nursing, rather than the measurement of outcomes. Brooking (1986) identified a scale to measure the use of the nursing process in hospital wards, the emphasis being on the process of care rather than the outcomes. The scale required observation of ward reports, admissions and nursing documentation. One could say that this approach is concerned with naturalism, that is, studying and evaluating nursing as it is, rather than attempting to manipulate it and quantify the outcomes. Within this approach one would expect to see observational techniques, in-depth interviewing and diary-keeping as a means of data collection to evaluate nursing care. Chenitz (1984) provided fascinating insights into the processes of nursing care from a qualitative perspective. She demonstrated, for example, how interaction could be analysed between a nurse expert in substance abuse and his or her patients. Table 5.1 reproduces a transcript of interaction with analysis and her identification of the processes involved. Clearly such a reflective and analytical approach to studying nursing care offers significant insights into evaluating that care.

In both these approaches to evaluation a number of issues should be raised as problematic. Firstly, in the quantitative approach to evaluation, Walton (1986) has stated that it is difficult, within multidisciplinary settings, to attribute outcomes of care purely to nursing staff. This is because other disciplines apart from nursing are involved in the care of people. Therefore, how can one attribute outcomes of care to one single discipline or person? Wilson Barnet (1981) has pointed out that there exist complex variables

Table 5.1 Analysis of Interaction (Chenitz 1984)

Interaction	Analysis	Processes
It is now 7.00 a.m.	Setting: Clinic. Context: early morning doses for working clients.	
Brenda Williams RN has been dispensing Methodone since 6.30 a.m.	Clinic opens at this time, the schedule being arranged for clients who hold jobs. Client-determined hours.	Dispensing (Clinic)
Joe S steps to the counter.	He has been waiting his turn. Methodone distributed at a counter, clients wait in other area.	Distributing (Clinic)
Without a word, Brenda interrupts her routine.	Why did she break routine? Selectively attending to something about this client.	Selectively attending (Patient)
She reaches for breathalyser and holds it up. Joe leans over and breathes into it. 'You're not doing too well'.	Problem related to alcohol use/abuse. Monitoring his alcohol. Not a word spoken.	Monitoring (Patient)
	Checked results evaluating this particular problem. She is concerned about this problem for him. Cannot dispense.	Evaluating (Patient)
'When are you going to see your counsellor?' she asks. He replies, 'I've got an appointment today'. 'Okay', Brenda says, as she passes him his daily dose of Methodone.	Protecting him from persisting or going unchecked with this problem.	Protecting (Patient)

that contribute to the disease process. There is, for example, evidence that factors beyond the control of the nurse contribute to, or hinder, recovery in patients. Clearly such factors will impinge upon the outcomes of the nursing care. The ability to separate out these factors from nursing care can prove problematic. Perhaps a purely 'outcome approach' assumes that, as long as one identifies the objectives of care, one can measure the outcomes and therefore make judgements of the care delivered. However, the world in which nurses work does not enable them to adopt such a simplistic stance.

Activity 5.1

The reader is asked to consider a plan of care for a patient or client which contains contributions to promoting or enabling advocacy. How could one identify those objectives which will have outcomes which could be measured? How could one identify and separate out the contributions made by the various disciplines involved in providing care?

One of the chief problems with the qualitative style of evaluation is that it relies upon subjective interpretations of events. Often a variety of data is used, for example, observation schedules, interviews and documentation. The wide use of different types of data often leads to cumbersome, lengthy descriptions of the nursing care provided. Some would argue that, compared with the presentation of quantitative data, this makes for an indigestible volume of data being put forward. There may also be a problem with the reliability and the validity of the data in qualitative evaluation. Some would argue that within this style of evaluation one may not be measuring what one originally set out to measure, and further, that if one measured the same process again, one would obtain entirely different results. Simply, the process, being subjective, is inherently unreliable and invalid. Again these criticisms represent a caricature of the problems of the qualitative approach to evaluation. This having been said, how do you think you might use a qualitative approach to evaluating the nursing care provided?

Activity 5.2

How might a nurse respond to a nurse manager, an administrator or a medical colleague, who, in response to a qualitative evaluation of nursing care, dismisses it as both unreliable and invalid?

Given the criticisms of both perspectives, it could be argued that it is important to adopt an approach that makes the best use of both styles of evaluation.

An Eclectic Approach

It can be seen from the preceding discussion that single theoretical perspectives often fail to address both the universal and complex natures of that which they seek to explain. Evaluation perspectives are no exception to this. Evaluation does not have to be an either/or scenario. In this chapter an eclectic approach is advocated, that is, a style that bases evaluation upon the use of a wide variety of data, methods for collecting that data and methods for analysing and making sense of that data. Because of the complexity of the task, McFarlane (1970) has advocated a 'sharing of approaches'.

Whichever method is used, it would seem important to adopt an approach that best answers the questions that are being asked. Evaluators often ask questions of a quantitative and qualitative nature at the same time. Therefore, more than one approach to answering such questions should be adopted. There is support within the literature

(Walton 1986 and Denzin 1978) for the suggestion that both the reliability and validity of evaluation can be significantly improved by using a wide variety of data and approaches to collecting, comparing and analysing that data. This process is referred to as **triangulation**. Walton (1986) has suggested that concentrating on outcomes without examining their cause could prove to be 'dangerously sterile'. This statement clearly supports the adoption of the eclectic approach that has already been advocated.

Now that the nature of evaluation has been briefly outlined, it is important to consider those aspects of advocacy that should be incorporated within the wider process of evaluating nursing care. In short, what should nurses evaluate? A single theoretical approach to evaluation is not advocated, neither in respect of the type of data that is collected, nor in how that data is obtained and used. This approach to evaluation promotes understanding of processes and may be undertaken either formatively or summatively. Clearly the process of nursing care is located within a world where variables other than nursing care impinge upon the total care process and therefore upon the nurse as advocate. These structural elements must be brought into an equation of evaluation. One cannot simply evaluate the provision and adequacy of advocacy within the framework of nursing care, without looking at the context in which that care was delivered.

Evaluation is now considered in relation to both the nurse practitioner's role as advocate and a collaborative nursing advocacy scheme.

Evaluating Self as Nurse Practitioner Advocate

This section clearly places the nurse in the centre of the process of evaluation. The reader will be asked to reflect upon and evaluate his or her practitioner skills connected with advocacy. This is not an easy task and at times it can become an uncomfortable exercise. However, it is suggested that nurses should attempt to be honest with themselves and seek to develop truly reflective skills concerning their practice. An exercise in 'armchair' evaluation is a good starting-point for individual assessment. This is achieved by the individual reflecting, away from the caring context, upon a reconstructed episode of patient care. Such a reconstruction requires readers to identify a person for whom they have recently cared in their role as nurse practitioner.

Activity 5.3

The reader should identify a patient who was in some way vulnerable, for example, in relation to his or her rights, interests, or the special nature of the nursing care provided. Having identified a person, the reader should then, without referring to this book, write a case history (a real one!), trying to capture as many of the details as can be remembered of their involvement in the care of that individual. The more accurate and realistic the case history, the more likely it is to invoke the experience encountered in caring for that person.

Having completed the case history, the reader can then return to the book and consider his or her contribution to the assessment, planning and implementation of the nursing care that the patient received. This will now be evaluated, under the stated headings, with particular reference to the adequacy of assessment and the need for an advocate or advocacy.

Assessment

This evaluation commences with identifying the adequacy, or otherwise, of the assessment of the person's immediate condition or circumstance and the broader aspects of being a person. Firstly, identify the major factors known at the time of assessment, for example:

1. Was a person being admitted to a surgical ward for an operation?
2. Was a person being seen at home, following a referral from the General Practitioner to the Community Psychiatric Nurse, for some mental health problem?
3. Was a child being admitted to a hospital ward for investigations for repeated seizures?
4. Was a person with a learning disability being seen at home because of the development of challenging behaviour?

Is it felt that such factors left them vulnerable in any way? Was there an attempt to stop and think whether that person might not receive a nurse's total care and support because of conflicting interests, for example with other disciplines? Did the nurse consider explaining that being an employee of a trust or health authority sometimes makes it extremely difficult to speak out for patients? If this was explained, was it also made clear that patients could, if they wished, either then or in the future, use the services of an advocate? If the service of an advocate was explained, how was this communicated? Was it recognised that such a proposal might have been problematic? Was there an attempt to assess the context or type of environment in which the nurse and the person were located? Was it possible to assess the type of advocate or advocacy service that the person required?

Clearly these questions provoke a range of responses that the reader may feel appropriate. However, perhaps it is the case that the value judgements that one now makes about the questions posed, encourage one to think of alternative, more effective strategies that could have been used in the assessment of the patient in relation to promoting their advocacy needs.

Planning

During the planning of the nursing care for a patient or client, were realistic goals, which incorporated a dimension of advocacy, set for that care? Was the collaborative planning of care with the patient or client based on how the latter might best use an advocacy service? If the patient concluded that some form of advocacy service was required and that you would act for him or her, did you identify within the planning process the potential personal threats that you might encounter as advocate and, if you did, how did you propose to manage them? In other words, how did you plan to manage your own support? In some instances within nursing care, patients do not require nurses to act as advocates for them. However, as we have discussed previously, it is perhaps inevitable that once a service is explained to patients then more will wish to take advantage of it.

Implementing

When implementing nursing care and at the same time advocating for a patient, nurses should be cognizant of their presentation of 'self' to others. Adversarial encounters seldom impress colleagues and generally create a more defensive environment in which a nurse must continue to work. Nurses should always attempt to try to use sensitive communication skills. During this exercise on evaluation the reader might like to reflect on how he or she communicated with colleagues. Was communication effective, were 'sound people-handling skills' demonstrated? Was the nurse able to interact with colleagues from a range of health and other agencies in an assertive manner, ensuring that interactions procured quality patient-centred care? Did the nurse use negotiating skills without any loss of composure? When evaluating the nursing care provided, a nurse sometimes needs to confront aspects that could, with hindsight, have been improved. In addition, nurses should consider the nature of the partnership between themselves and their patient. Without a clearly understood partnership, advocacy would be almost impossible to pursue. Somewhere within the evaluation of the implementation of nursing care, nurses must ask themselves whether they enabled the development of a true partnership. This is different from the perpetuation of parentalistic care, which is where a nurse may have treated, perhaps unintentionally, the patient or client like a small child, as if nurse knew best.

Within this section a number of questions have been posed and a number of avenues outlined for nurses to pursue in evaluating their nursing care related to advocacy.

Evaluating a Collaborative Advocacy Scheme of Nurses

This next section pursues the model of collaborative advocacy outlined in chapter 4, and explores the evaluation of this proposed model. The work of O'Brien (1987) is used extensively with particular reference to his writing on citizen advocacy programme evaluation standards, based upon CAPE (Citizen Advocacy Programme Evaluation). Nursing must be committed to evaluating its contribution and to the promotion of advocacy from both individual practitioner and organisational perspectives. The principle of improving practice through evaluation is just as valid for the organisation as for an individual.

Let us assume that a number of nursing colleagues have formed themselves into a voluntary, independent collaborative advocacy scheme. They have based their scheme on the broad principles of citizen advocacy (the reader may wish to revise the proposed model that was outlined in chapter 4). The scheme they have developed may be accessed either by nurse practitioners wishing to refer their patients or by the patients themselves, its overriding aim being to 'provide independent nursing advocacy, for a range of people who require someone to represent their interests or rights'.

The scheme has been running for approximately six months and they now wish to evaluate how successful their attempts at achieving this aim have been. The reasons for this evaluation having been outlined, it might be appropriate to restate the principles of citizen advocacy and sketch out methods by which the nurses could conduct their evaluation. There are a number of fundamental principles upon which citizen advocacy is based, and these are broadly applicable to the proposed collaborative advocacy scheme of the nurses:

- The first of these principles is the creation of relationships that support and represent the interests of individuals who are in need of an advocate.
- The second principle is that an advocate enters such a relationship or partnership freely and through a desire to support an individual in difficult times.
- The penultimate principle is that the advocacy scheme should promote positive interactions and imagery of all people, regardless of their disability.
- The last principle is that the scheme should be clearly defined within the community that it serves. Within this principle it is assumed that the scheme is able to function independently of human service delivery systems.

In order for a nurse to evaluate an established collaborative advocacy scheme, it is necessary to measure the processes and outcomes of the scheme against some predetermined standards. This does not exclude the qualitative style of evaluation, nor the formative timing to the process. Both these elements will obviously contribute to a much richer and insightful evaluation. O'Brien (1987) successfully managed to combine qualitative, quantitative, summative and formative elements within a single approach to evaluation.

The remainder of this section outlines this particular approach to evaluating an advocacy service and is based upon the standards used by the CAPE system. The CAPE format is divided into four sections, which respectively examine:

1. the commitment of the scheme to the principles of citizen advocacy,
2. the concept of learning from citizen advocacy relationships,
3. the area of learning from the citizen advocate co-ordinator, and
4. the programme's foundations and structure.

In the methodology for the programme it is proposed that a team be established to conduct the evaluation. The proposed team should use the expertise of an experienced evaluator in CAPE methodology. Each of the four sections is now considered in greater depth.

Commitment to citizen advocacy principles

This first section of the CAPE format identifies a check list of standards related to the principles of advocacy, requiring an evaluation team to answer a yes/no statement. There is also space provided for the team to record evidence or additional notes to the responses made. This lends a more qualitative component to the nominal data of 'yes' or 'no' and is important when the team reflects on its findings, because it reminds the evaluation team of the context in which the value judgements of the advocacy scheme were made. The team is also invited to note contradictions to the principles of advocacy and to record developments and compromises, so that comparisons between repeated evaluations may be made. This is important because if, in an evaluation, practices that contradict the principles of advocacy emerge, then one would expect that, by the time of the next re-evaluation, the scheme would have been improved and developed. This brings us to the important area of setting agendas for action. If contradictions or compromises that require attention and modification are found within a scheme, then it is important that an agenda be established for deciding 'how' and 'when' modifications in the practice of the scheme will be made in order to reduce, minimise or eradicate such contradictions. The evaluation team is expected to use all comments to produce an agenda based on action priorities. Below are examples of possible standards and formats, based on CAPE, that could be used for recording contradictions, compromises and the setting of an agenda for action. These may prove helpful to the reader in consolidating the what, when and where of evaluation. Table 5.2 states a fundamental principle of citizen advocacy, followed by a number of questions that will evidence whether the scheme is operating within this ideological framework. It can be seen that the evaluation team is required simply to respond 'yes' or 'no'.

Nurses from the collaborative scheme enter a relationship that is independent of human service systems and is not controlled by the advocacy scheme.

Table 5.2. Fundamental principle of advocacy and questions of fidelity.

- Nurses give their time and share their personal resources without pay or any form of compensation.   Yes/No
- The collaborative scheme encourages nurse advocates to find direction in their relationships. Within the programme, nurses are supported but not supervised or evaluated.   Yes/No

- The scheme encourages nurse advocates to   Yes/No
  explore new ways of resolving difficult situations.
- If a nurse advocate is matched with a patient, client   Yes/No
  or protégé where the partnership is not developing,
  there is a mechanism for dealing with this issue.

Table 5.3 enables the evaluation team to record more qualitative elements of this exercise. There are spaces for
recording positive instances of practice that promote advocacy, for evidence of contradictions to the ideology of
advocacy and for suggestions on how such contradictions
can be improved.

Table 5.3. Positive findings and contradictions to citizen
advocacy

Positive instances in which the concept and practice of advocacy
are being implemented by the scheme:

1

2

3

Evidence of practice that contradicts advocacy:

1

2

3

Suggestions by the evaluation team for improvement:

1

2

3

Table 5.4 enables the team to identify developments in the scheme since its last evaluation. It is often the case that practices driven by a strong underlying ideology need to compromise those ideals in order to make a scheme work. It can be seen that space has been provided for the evaluation team to record a rationale for making such compromises. This enables the team to make a value judgement as to the appropriateness of the compromise.

Table 5.4. Developments and compromises of the scheme

Developments and compromises

This space should be used by the evaluation team to summarise ways in which advocacy principles have had to be changed or modified in order to make the scheme work.

This space should be used by the evaluation team to summarise the reasons for changing any advocacy principles to facilitate the working of the scheme.

Table 5.5 shows a proposed format for setting out an agenda for action. It can be seen that a time element has been built in for development of the scheme, as well as instructions for establishing priorities for action.

Table 5.5. An agenda for action

Agenda for action

This sheet should be used by the evaluation team to identify the issues that are most critical in the scheme's development. Consideration should be given to:

1. The agenda for the following year, aimed at building a stronger advocacy programme.

2. Immediate threats, if any, to the scheme's integrity.

Learning from citizen advocacy relationships

This second section explores the nature of the relationships between the advocate and protégé. The purpose of this section is for the evaluators to interview both the advocate and protégé to form impressions of how relationships are initiated and supported. The emphasis is not upon the relationships themselves, but on the advocacy scheme. The interviewers from the evaluation team are required to make interview notes during the interview or compile a summary at the end of the interview. An example is provided in table 5.6 of some proposed statements an evaluator would rate on a 'Lickert type' rating scale, which would form the interview summary. It can be seen that statements are provided with a scale from 1 to 5. 1 represents strong disagreement or 'never' and 5 strong agreement or 'always'. It should be noted that 5 does not necessarily describe the best situation. Best implies there is a single answer, but both advocate and protégé may

Table 5.6. Advocacy relationships

| Circle the appropriate number against each statement. | 1 = Strongly disagree / Never
2 = Mostly disagree / Seldom
3 = Sometimes agree / Occasionally
4 = Mostly agree / Mostly
5 = Strongly agree / Always |

- The nurse advocate has a clear idea of what is in the best interests of the person.   1 2 3 4 5
- The nurse advocate acts vigorously in representing the person.   1 2 3 4 5
- The nurse advocate uses her personal network on behalf of the person.   1 2 3 4 5
- The nurse advocate attempts to understand the person's world.   1 2 3 4 5
- The nurse advocate attempts to get more or different human service delivery systems.   1 2 3 4 5
- The nurse advocate has made known the person's situation to community groups.   1 2 3 4 5
- The nurse advocate has, as a result of the partnerships, become more involved in the concerns of the community in which she lives.   1 2 3 4 5

disagree as to which is acceptable and reflects the nature of a true partnership.

This section also seeks to illuminate patterns in the advocacy scheme. For example, how well is the scheme doing with initiating and supporting relationships, expanding the range of relationships and improving the process of recruiting advocates?

The evaluation team is next required to study the scheme's statistics. By this it is meant that the evaluation team should make value judgements on, for example, the number of partnerships established and successful outcomes of relationships. It is possible that the team may identify that the scheme does not maintain statistical data (not uncommon), in which case it is likely that there is a need to promote this as an area for development within the scheme. The team should also consider age distribution, the range of disability and need for advocacy. Finally, in relation to all the information gathered from this section the team is required to study the data and identify:

1. What the team has learnt from the individuals met, and

2. What the scheme could do to become more effective.

Learning from the citizen advocate co-ordinator

This third section concentrates on the co-ordination of the scheme. Within the model of a collaborative advocacy scheme run by nurses, it is improbable, but not impossible, that one single person would wish to accept overall responsibility for the co-ordination of the scheme. Consider recently retired nursing staff, perhaps nursing staff who have left the profession for reasons of ill health or who have retired early. Individuals such as these may be willing to contribute to the development of a scheme able to offer 'true' care for all people in need of advocacy. This said, the section should probably be viewed as focusing on a number of people who would share a co-ordinating responsibility. It concentrates on recruitment, matching advocates and protégés, support to advocates and the role of the co-ordinator(s). A number of sections are provided for the evaluation team to record their findings obtained through interviews. These findings are then compared to the principles of citizen advocacy. Table 5.7 provides one example of a proposed format that the evaluation team could use when looking at the co-ordinator's role in relation to the scheme.

Table 5.7. The Co-ordinator

How the co-ordinator undertakes matching nurses and partners.
Current difficulties experienced by co-ordinator.
Consistency of co-ordination with advocacy principles.

Learning about citizen advocacy programme foundations and structures

The last section of this evaluation strategy, as its title implies, seeks to explore both the foundations and structures of the advocacy scheme. For example, the evaluation team is required to look at the scheme's constitution, minutes of meetings and annual reports, and in addition would be expected to study funding arrangements, if any. Again, amongst the various formats for collecting this information (see table 5.8), there is a proposed 'Lickert type' rating scale to measure and arrive at an overall impression and conclusion as to the scheme's foundations and structure. 1 is indicative of strong disagreement or 'never' and 5 of strong agreement or 'always'.

Within this section of the book an approach to evaluation has been outlined at the organisational level of definition. The collaborative scheme of advocacy proposed is now fully developed. The model (see chapter 4) includes a proposed rationale, probable constitution, operational methods and evaluation strategies of its practice. Such a model has the potential to promote and extend the caring capacity of nurses, which is so often thwarted within the context of their work settings. The final section of this book briefly recounts and brings to a conclusion the discussions concerning advocacy and nursing.

Table 5.8. The scheme's structure

| The collaborative scheme's structure
Circle the appropriate number against each statement. | 1 = Strongly disagree / Never
2 = Mostly disagree / Seldom
3 = Sometimes agree / Occasionally
4 = Mostly agree / Mostly
5 = Strongly agree / Always |

- The scheme's structure is independent of service delivery systems.   1 2 3 4 5
- The scheme has a clear constitution.   1 2 3 4 5
- All steering committee members are independent of service delivery systems.   1 2 3 4 5
- The scheme has clearly defined areas of expertise.   1 2 3 4 5
- The committee maintains minutes of all the scheme's formal meetings.   1 2 3 4 5
- An annual report of all the scheme's activities is prepared.   1 2 3 4 5
- The scheme has created public awareness of its activities   1 2 3 4 5

Reflections on a Journey Through Advocacy

The book commenced with a selective exploration of the literature on advocacy and by defining what advocacy is and what advocacy is about. The view has been put forward, and consistently argued throughout the book, that for a nurse to act as advocate is at best difficult and at worst dangerous. This is because of conflicting loyalties, role conflict, environmental or contextual factors, as well as a range of ethical issues. However, it has also been argued that a nurse can and should act as advocate, but that this decision should be made by individual nurse practitioners. What is important is that nurses are not compelled to act as advocates, but instead are capable of using their nursing skills to network and refer patients to advocacy schemes or other practitioners in order to bring about advocate partnerships.

Successful and unsuccessful projects have been described that led to the recognition of types of environment in which nurses work. Before adopting the role of advocate, a nurse should have an understanding of these contexts as a basis for decision-making. Shortcomings in the ways in which advocacy and the skills of advocacy are taught have been discussed. This led to an outline of an alternative model for students of nursing to be able to learn about advocacy.

In chapter 4 a new collaborative scheme for nursing advocacy was described. It is proposed that this would enable nurses to reclaim their legitimate role in caring for people in the widest sense, as compared with merely attending to the 'cosmetic' needs of patients or clients. Lastly, within this chapter two levels of definition of evaluation have been described.

To conclude, the essence of advocacy is the unshackling of people from their worries, concerns and difficulties, through partnerships but without parentalism, by contributing to their own empowerment to experience the world, in the best state of health possible for them.

References

Abrams N (1978) A contrary view of the nurse as patient advocate. *Nursing Forum*, **XVII** (3): 259–67.

Audit Commission (1991) *The Virtue of Patients: Making better use of ward nursing resources*. London: HMSO.

Binnie A (1982) A report of the nursing process pilot project. Cambridge Health Authority. In Hayward J (1986) *Report of the Nursing Process Evaluation Group.* NERU Report no. 5. London: Kings College University of London.

Brooking J (1986) *Patient and Family Participation in Nursing Care: The development of a nursing process measuring scale.* Unpublished PhD thesis, Kings College University of London.

Chenitz C (1984) Surfacing nursing process. A method for generating nursing theory from practice. *Journal of Advanced Nursing,* 9: 205–15.

Denzin N (1978) The logic of the naturalistic enquiry. In Denzin N (ed.) *Sociological Methods: A source book.* New York: McGraw Hill.

Hawthorn P (1984) Measuring change in nursing practice. *Journal of Advanced Nursing,* **9** (3): 239–47.

Luker K (1981) An overview of evaluation research in nursing. *Journal of Advanced Nursing,* **6** (1): 87–93.

McFarlane J (1970) *The Proper Study of the Nurse.* London: Royal College of Nursing.

McKinley S (1986) An advocacy role for the critical care nurse. *The Australian Journal of Advanced Nursing,* **4** (1): 3–12.

Miller A (1984) Nursing process and patient care. *Nursing Times,* Occasional Papers, **80** (13): 56–8.

O'Brien J (1987) Learning from Citizen Advocacy Programmes. Sections 1–5. USA: Georgia Advocacy Office.

Walton I (1986) *The Nursing Process in Perspective.* A literature review. York: University of York, Department of Social Policy and Social Work.

Whitfield S (1985) The end of the beginning. City and Hackney Health Authority. In Hayward J (1986) *Report of the Nursing Process Evaluation Group.* NERU Report no. 5. London: Kings College University of London.

Wilson Barnet J (1981) Reason for selecting care. Janforum. *Journal of Advanced Nursing,* **6** (6): 508.

Index